ANCIENT HISTORY
OF THE
DECCAN

ANCIENT HISTORY
OF THE
DECCAN

G. JOUVEAU-DUBREUIL

TRANSLATED FROM FRENCH BY
V.S. SWAMINADHA DIKSHITAR

GYAN

Published by

Gyan Publishing House
5, Ansari Road
Daryaganj, New Delhi-110002
Phone: 011-47034999, 9811692060
E-mail: books@gyanbooks.com

Distribution Network
gyanbooks.com
India, USA, Canada, UK, Australia, France

ISBN : 978-81-212-3121-3 (PB)
First Published, Pondicherry, 1920

2nd Impression 2020

Printed at: Gyan Press, Delhi.

Ancient History of the Deccan
Author: G. Jouveau-Dubreuil

ANCIENT HISTORY
OF THE
DECCAN

BY

G. JOUVEAU-DUBREUIL
Doctor of the University of Paris,
Professor, College, Pondicherry.

TRANSLATED FROM FRENCH
BY

V. S. SWAMINADHA DIKSHITAR, B.A., L.T.,
Officier d'Académie
Professor of English, Colonial College, Pondicherry.

PONDICHERRY:
SOLD BY THE AUTHOR
6, DUMAS STREET.

1920

ABBREVIATIONS.

A. D.	Anno Domini (After Christ).
A. S. W. I.	Archæological Survey Western India.
B. C.	Before Christ.
Ep. Carn.	Epigraphia Carnatica (Rice).
Ep. Ind.	Epigraphia Indica, Calcutta.
Ind. Ant.	Indian Antiquary, Bombay.
J. B. B. R. A. S.	Journal of the Bombay branch of the Royal Asiatic Society.
J. R. A. S.	Journal of the Royal Asiatic Society.
Lüders's list.	List of inscriptions in Ep. Ind. Vol. X.
Rapson.	Catalogue of the coins of the Andhra dynasty, the Western Ksatrapas, etc, in the British Museum, by Prof. Rapson, London.

INTRODUCTION

India may be divided into two parts, the North and the South. From the remotest times, this division has been adopted by the Indians who have given the name of Dakshiṇa (Dakshiṇâpatha) or 'The South' to all the Country that extends from the Narbadà to the extremity of the peninsula. In this work, we shall use the word Deccan to designate the ancient Dakshiṇa, but with this little restriction, that the three Southernmost kingdoms of Chôḷa, Chêra and Pâṇḍya, which have always remained a little isolated, shall be excluded. We shall therefore call "The Deccan" the large tract of country which is bounded on the north by the Narbadâ and the Mahânadi, on the east by the Bay of Bengal, on the west by the Arabian Sea, on the south by the Nilgiri Hills and the Southern Peṇṇâr (which reaches the sea near Cuddalore and which is the northern boundary of the Chôḷa country according to the poetess Auvaiyàr).

We have limited our subject in extent; let us now proceed to fix a time-limit for it. "Ancient History of the Deccan" means for us "the history of the Deccan in ancient times" and the words "ancient times" denotes the 9 centuries extending from 261 B. C, to about 610 A. D, that is to say, from Aśôka to Pulakêśin II. In fact, we have no historical document anterior to Aśôka; and so we shall begin our history from the time of this king, about 261 B. C, (the Kaliṅga war). On the other hand, from the time of Pulakêśin II, about 610 A. D, we have a large number of historical documents and the history of the Deccan is mostly known. It is therefore this historic period between 261 B. C, and 610 A. D, that is denoted by the words, "Deccan in Ancient times" and that we are going to study in this work.

The only book in which we find some information on their subject is the "Bombay Gazetteer" Vol. I. Part II (1896) which contains two works: "Early History of the Deccan" by R. G. Bhandarkar and "Dynasties of the Kanarese Districts" by J. F Fleet. This book is well-known and there is no need to praise it here. But to-day it has one defect: it is twenty-five years old and during this last quarter of a century numerous discoveries have been made and "The Bombay Gazetteer" Vol. I. Part II. is not at all "up to date". Besides, this book itself does not contain, strictly speaking, the history of the Deccan in ancient times. The portion concerning the ancient times is very succinct, for, in 1896, the number of documents concerning it was small. Moreover, the Bombay Presidency does not by itself constitute the whole of the Deccan.

We may therefore say that today the History of the Deccan is quite a new subject. The student who wishes to know what was the History of the Deccan between 261 B. C, and 610 A. D, does not know what books to consult. This history is lost in obscurity. Still it is not the documents that are wanting; for the dynasty of the Kadambas alone, we have about thirty copper-plates. We have also plentv of information about the Pallavas and the Gangas. Why then is the chronology of these dynasties so mysterious? I thought that what was wanted most at the present time was to arrange the parts and make a whole work of it; I thought that a complete and attentive study of all the documents we actually possess will throw a flood of light on the darkness, bring order out of chaos and, in short, give birth to, what we have not had up to the present, the Ancient History of the Deccan.

Such a study is very important, as it is the history of nine glorious centuries of this large country. The documents that we have concerning the Deccan of the ancient times enable us to conclude that all this period was one of high civilisation and historical celebrity. We shall see that during the epoch of Aśôka, the Deccan was not at all uncivilised. The art of writing was known a long time before it and the inscriptions of Aśôka were read and understood very well at that time. From a military point of view, the Deccan was never more powerful than at the time of Śâtakarṇis who, without doubt, succeeded many times in vanquishing the kings of the northern countries and annexing a part of their territories, From a sculptural point of view, the Deccan, like the North. was inspired by the Greek and Roman arts and the marbles of Amarâvatî can be compared to the sculptures of Gandhara. If now we consider the monuments, the Deccan is much superior to the North. If we compare the ancient monuments of Northern and Southern India we find that the North is relatively poor. In the Deccan there is a very large number of sculptured rocks at Udayagiri, Junnar, Ellora, Nâsik, Kaṇhêri etc. And speaking only of the chief of them, which are the monuments in the north that will bear comparison with the grand Chaitya at Kârli that is equal in its dimensions to the Gothic Cathedrals, or with the monasteries of Ajaṇṭâ with their marvellous painting? There is, it is true, the great Stûpa at Sâñchi, but this monument is in Bhilsa near Deccan; it may even be considered a monument of the Deccan, since its balustrade which is the cause of all its celebrity has been sculptured, as is evident from an inscription, by the workmen of one Śâtakarṇi, that is to say, a king of the Deccan. Writing the history of the Deccan therefore means writing the history of the most remarkable monuments of India.

If we look at a map we find that the Deccan is an immense country, almost one half of India. If we examine the monuments, we shall have the certainty that this country has enjoyed a high degree of civilisation and if we bear in mind that the history of the Deccan in ancient times is the history of nine glorious centuries, we cannot but conclude that this history is well worth studying and that it must come out of the almost complete obscurity in which it has remained up to the present day.

This book is up to date as far as the documents available in India up to the end of 1919 are concerned.

CHAPTER I.

THE EARLY KINGS

§ 1. Aśôka.

One of the well-known events in the history of Aśôka is the conquest of Kalinga which probably took place about 261 B. C. and it is not astonishing to find an inscription of Aśôka at Dhaulî. This town situated in the delta of the Mahânadi is in all probability the ancient Tosalî, capital of the kingdom of Kalinga; for, according to Mr. Haraprashad Sastri, Tosalî is etymologically identical with Dhaulî. It is not more astonishing that there is another inscription at Jaugada (Ganjam District, Madras Presidency), as this place certainly formed part of the kingdom of Kalinga (concerning the Kalinga edicts, see Ind. Ant., Vol V, pp. 82-102; see also Arch. Surv. Southern India, Amarâvatî, by Burgess, pp. 114-25).

The discovery of an inscription at Sopârâ (Thânâ District, Bombay Presidency) near Bombay, has proved that the north-west of the Deccan as well as the north-east where Kalinga is situated has been under the domination of Aśôka. But the discovery, in 1892, of the inscriptions of Aśôka near Siddâpura, in Mysore, which have immortalised the name of Mr. Rice, has caused very great surprise. They did not, in fact, think that the empire of Aśôka extended up to the southernmost part of the Deccan. One very important point in the history of India was thus well established. So, the discovery, (see Hyderabad Archælogical Series No 1) only a few years ago, of an inscription at Mâski (Lingsugur Taluq, Raichur District) in the State of Hyderabad has caused no surprise.

The Siddâpura edicts (near Brahmagiri, in Molakâlmuru taluk; see Ep. Carn. Vol. XI, MK, 21, 14, 34, and Mysore and Coorg from inscriptions by Mr. Rice, page 11; see also Fleet, J. R. A. S., for 1903, page 829 and J. R. A. S., for 1904, pages 1 and 355) present certain peculiarities which have been pointed out by Bühler and especially "the particular uncouth form of "ma" with its abnormally large upper limbs" (which re-occurs in the inscriptions on the crystal prism from the Bhaṭṭiprôlu stûpa, Ep. Ind. Vol. III. page 135). These details are very important. One is indeed led to believe that the edicts were engraved by the emissaries of Aśôka who came from the north, but that the people of those distant countries, where the edicts were published, understood very little of those inscriptions that were written in a language and an alphabet almost unknown to them. We may also suppose that at the time of Aśôka the people of Mysore were almost savages. On the contrary, the Siddâpura inscriptions prove that South India had a special alphabet which Bühler has called "Drâviḍî" and that the art of writing was known many centuries before Aśôka, for, in the III century B.C. the alphabet of the South has had time to vary from that of the North. Besides, the special alphabet used in the Siddâpura inscriptions proves that the edicts of Aśôka were engraved by some Southerners who must therefore have understood the language of Aśôka and attained as high a degree of civilisation as the northerners.

It is almost certain that Aśôka led only one expedition, that to Kaliṅga. But how did the rest of the Deccan come under his domination? It is to be supposed that, at the accession of Aśôka, the whole of the Deccan except Kaliṅga was already in the possession of the Mauryas. There are also, in Mysore, certain legends about the Mauryan king Chandragupta (see "Mysore and Coorg from inscriptions" by Mr. Rice). We may also suppose that the rest of the Deccan quietly submitted on hearing of the conquest of Kaliṅga. Be it as it may, it is certain that the whole of the Deccan was under the suzerainty of Aśôka and that, consequently, the political unity of India was a *fait accompli*, twenty-two centuries ago.

§ 2. Kubêra of Bhaṭṭiprôlu.

In the year 1892, Mr. A. Rea deposited in the Madras Museum six large stones of the caskets that he had discovered in the centre of the dome of the stûpa at Bhaṭṭiprôlu (Repalle taluk, Guntûr District) near the mouth of the Kṛishṇâ (see G. O., 18th June 1892, No. 423). These inscriptions were written in an alphabet which Bühler (page 39 of the Appendix of Ind. Ant. Vol. XXXIII) considers to be very old: "immediately after Aśôka or about B. C. 200" (see J. R. A. S., 1892, p. 602. "A new variety of the Southern Maurya Alphabet by G. Bühler"). One of these inscriptions (No. 1338 of Lüders's List) says that "at that time, Kubiraka (Kubêraka) was king" (see Bühler, Ep. Ind. Vol. II, p. 323).

We know nothing more about this king Kubêra; we do not know the name of the dynasty to which he belonged and the extent of his kingdom.

§ 3. Khâravela of Kaliṅga.

The Udayagiri hill is situated nineteen miles south of Cuttack in Orissa. The Jains have cut many caves there. One of them called Hâtigumphâ contains a famous inscription which has been decently copied and studied only in 1917 (See Journal of the Bihar and Orissa Research Society, Vol. III, December 1917, pp. 425-507)

This inscription dated the 165th year of "ràja-muriyakâle" which corresponds to the 13th year of the reign of Khâravêla, king of Kaliṅga, gives us very valuable information about the reign of this king. He belongs to the Cheta dynasty; he vanquihed Śâtakarṇi and forced Bahapati, king of Râjagṛiha to flee to Mathurâ. Besides, the inscriptions in the Manchapuri cave (see Ep. Ind. Vol. XIII, p. 159, No. 13) mention (insc. No. I) the chief queen of Khâravela who was the daughter of King Lâlâka, the grandson of Hastisâha (insc. No. II), the king of Kaliṅga Kûdêpasiri and (insc. No. III) the prince Vaḍukha.

The date 165 will be of very great value if we knew exactly the origin of the era that has been employed; unfortunately we have to remain content with a supposition; it is however probable that this era dates from the coronation of Chandragupta and in that case the year 165 will correspond to 157 B.C.

The reading and the translation of the Khâravela inscription as given by Messrs. R. D. Banerji and K. P. Jayaswal, is open to some criticism; Mr. R. C. Majumdar (Ind. Ant. Vol. XLII, Aug. 1918, pp. 223 and 224) has contested many of these conclusions (see also: "Khâravela" by Ramâprasâd Chanda in J. R. A. S., July 1919, page 395). However, Mr. Vincent A. Smith (J. R. A. S. for 1918, page 543, "New light on Ancient India") has admitted that king Bahapati can be identified with Pushyamitra and with Bahasatimitra of the coins and inscriptions, and he places the epoch of Pushyamitra in about 160 B. C.

The synchronism of Śâtakarṇi and Khâravela with Pushyamitra is enough, by itself, to establish approximately the date of the ancient kings of the Deccan.

§ 4. The earliest Sâtavâhana kings.

No. 1. Śâtakarṇi of Nânâghâṭ.— Nânâghâṭ is a defile (the Nana pass) in the mountains to the east of Bombay. There is here a chamber cut in the rock to serve probably as a place of shelter for travellers. The walls of this cave contain inscriptions (No. 1112 of Lüders's list in Ep. Ind. Vol. X) and further there are remnants of some bas-reliefs representing certain personages. These bas-reliefs contain explanatory legends (Nos. 1113, 1114, 1115, 1116, 1117, 1118 of Lüders's list). From these inscriptions Bühler (A. S. W. I., Vol. V, p. 66) has drawn the following conclusions: Śâtakarṇi, king of Dakshiṇapatha and son of Simuka of the Sâtavâhana dynasty gained many victories and performed the horse-sacrifice (Aśvamedha) twice. After his death, his wife Nâganikâ daugther of Mahârathi [Tra]nakayiro [Kaḷa] lâya, the scion of the Angira family, was proclaimed regent during the minority of the princes, the elder called Vediśri and the younger Śakti-Śri (Sati-Srimat) or Haku-Śri. Here we have to note that an inscription at Nâsik (No. 1141 of Lüders's list) mentions the granddaughter of Mahàhakuśri (Ep. Ind. Vol. VIII, p. 91). As prince Hakuśri was but a child at the time when the Nânâghâṭ inscriptions were written and his granddaughter was an elderly woman at the time of the Nâsik inscription (her son Kapaṇaṇaka was probably a man at this time) the two Haku-Śris may be dentified with each other by supposing that there was an interval of about a century between the two inscriptions. The palæography of the inscriptions seems in fact to indicate nearly this difference in age.

The alphabet of the inscriptions in the Nânâghâṭ cave seems almost to belong to the same epoch as that of the Khâravela inscription; and all the authors have admitted the possibility of identifying Śâtakarṇi of Nânâghâṭ with the one mentioned in the Khâravela inscription.

No. 2. Krishṇa of Nâsik.— In Nâsik there is a small cave which seems to be the most ancient of all this group of excavations that are found in this place. An inscription (No. 1144 of Lüders's list and Ep. Ind. Vol. VIII, p. 93) tells us that it was caused to be made by an inhabitant of Nâsik in the time of Râjan Kânha (Krishṇa) of the Śadavâhana family. The alphabet of this inscription is analogous to that of the Nânâgaṭ and Udayagiri inscriptions.

We must mention here that according to the Purâṇas the dynasty of the Ândhras (Śâtavâhanas) was founded by a king name Śiśuka, who had as his successors his brother Krishṇa and a third king called Sâtakarṇi. The name Śiśuka is possibly a modified form of the name Simuka that we find in Nânâghâṭ, that his brother Krishṇa was he of Nâsik and that Śâtakarṇi was the one of Nânâghâṭ.

No. 3. Śâtakarṇi of Sâñchi.— The grand Stûpa at Sâñchi which dates from Aśôka has been restored and embellished at different times. The most interesting part of it is undoubtedly the balustrade which has four magnificently ornamented gateways. The oldest of them (Archæological Survey of India; Report for 1913-1914, page 6) is the one in the south. It is also the only one that contains an inscription in which the name of a king is mentioned and this name, strange to say, is Śâtakarṇi. This inscription says, in fact, that an image is due to the sculptor of the great king Śâtakarṇi. Unfortunately, this name has been borne by a great number of Śâtavâhana kings. We are however glad to have the certainty that this dynasty extended its empire up to Bhilsâ, namely the antique Vidiśa, and that it was precisely under this dynasty that one of the most celebrated monuments of India was sculptured. The inscription has been reproduced only in fac-simile in Cunningham's "Bhilsâ Topes" where it figures as No. 190. Bühler has formed the following Judgment (Ep. Ind. Vol. II. p. 88) on the characters of the inscription: "they are almost identical with those of the Nânàghâṭ inscriptions, and differ only slightly from the type of the characters of Aśôka times."

There can therefore be no question of identifying this Sâtakarṇi with the later king Gautamiputra though this king probably reigned not far from Śâñchi. The characters of our inscription are much too archaic. We cannot also identify this Śâtakarṇi with those of the Udayagiri or Nânâghâṭ inscriptions, for it was Pushyamitra that reigned at Bhilsâ at this time. When, then, did Śâtakarṇi of Sâñchi reign ? It is probable that Bhilsâ, which was under the Mauryas passed directly into the hands of the Śungas. It was the capital of the viceroy Agnimitra. We are sure (Archæological Survey of India Report for 1908-1909, page 127) that later on Kâutsiputra-Bhâgabhadra was the king of Vidiśa (Bhilsâ) and a contemporary of Antialkidas. If the Besnagar inscriptions, to which we allude, mean by Kâsiputra Bhâgabhadra the 9th Suṅga king, there is no doubt that Bhilsâ remained in the possession of this dynasty till the 10th king, Devabhûmi, the successor of Bhâgavata (Bhâgabhadra) was murdered by Vasudêva Kâṅva.

It is not impossible that a Śâtavâhana helped Vasudêva in his usurpation and so appropriated the country of Bhîlsâ to himself. It must have taken place about 72 B. C. Besides, it is very probable that the Śakas invaded northern India in the middle of the 1st century before our era; it is possible that this great conquest took place about 58. B. C; at this epoch the Sâtavâhanas would have been driven not only from Bhilsâ but also out of Mahârâshtra. There is therefore room to think that the Śâtakarṇi who is mentioned on the Sâñchi gateway reigned at Bhilsâ between 72 B.C. and 58 B. C. or in round figures from 70 to 60 B. C. I think that ths alphabet of the inscription and the style of the sculpturee accord with each other to justify this date.

The most ancient conis of the dynasty of Śâtavâhanas have been found in western India and are of the type that Mr. Rapson calls Mâḷwâ fabric and which he thinks is "connected with the early east and punch-marked coins of Eran" (see Rapson: "coins of Ândhra dynasty" page 1, Nos. 1 and 2). These coins represent an elephant and a river and bear the inscription "Srî Sata" We may think that this king reigned at an epoch which is very close to that of Śâtakarṇi of Sâñchi.

CHAPTER II.

THE ŚAKA PERIOD OF THE HISTORY OF THE DECCAN

§ 1. The Kshaharâtas.

To understand the history of the Deccan in the 1st century B. C. and the first two centuries A. D., we must know the history of the whole of India at this epoch; but that history is very uncertain even today; and we do not wish to force a theory upon our readers but intend only to set forth our personal opinion on this subject.

In the II century B. C. the Śaka tribe that came from the north entered into Northern India; from that time they were intimately connected with another tribe, the Parthians, and had close relationship with Persia. In the history of India, the names of Śakas, Pahlavas and Yavanas are mentioned simultaneously and denote those foreigners that came from the north-western frontier. It is probably about 100 B. C. that one of these princes reigned at Taxila under the name of Maues. Later on, about 60 B. C., Azes. I ascended the throne. This king probably had a long and glorious reign. It was perhaps in his time that the Parthians and the Sakas conquered almost the whole of northern India and a portion of the Deccan. When the Indo-Parthian kings Azes I, Azilises, Azes II, Gondopharnes were reigning over the Panjâb, the rest of the empire was governed by more or less independent princes who bore the title of Kshatrâpas and Mahâkshatrapaa. In the province surrounding the Gulf of Cambay (Surâshtrs,

Ujjain, Aparânta) there reigned the Śaka kings who were called Bhûmaka and Nahapâna. The Śakas called Hagâna, Hagâmâsha, Râjuvula, Śodâsa, Kharahostes and Kalni reigned at Mathurâ in the valley of the Ganges. The Śakas (Bhûmaka, Nahapãna) that reigned over the country round the Gulf of Cambay (in Surâshṭra, Ujjain and Northern Deccan) belonged to the same family as the Śakas (Râjûvula, Śodâsa) of Mathurâ; this family was that of the Kshaharâtas. In fact, the Nâsik inscriptions say that the Śakas who reigned in Northern Deccan belonged to the dynasty of the Kshaharâtas and, they have discovered in 1910-1911 at Gaṇêshrâ (3 miles west of Mathurâ, in mound No. 2 (See J. R. A. S., year 1912, p. 122) a fragment of an inscription (fig. II, plate II) which contains clearly the word "Kshaharâtasa".

Professor Rapson, who discovered the existence of the name Bhûmaka on the coins, has written: "considerations of "the type and fabric of the coins, and of the nature of the coin "legends leave no room for doubting that Bhûmaka preceded "Nahapâna" (Rapson, coins of the Ândhra dynasty, page CVIII). These coins bear as insignia, either "the arrow, discus and thunderbolt" or "the Lion capital and Dharmachakra." "The "coins of Bhûmaka seem to supply an important link between "the bronze coins of Nahapâna and those struck conjointly "by the Pahlava Spalirises and the Śaka Azes" (J. R. A. S. for 1904, p. 372). The insignia 'Discus, Bow and Arrow' connect these coins with those of Azes I: "It may be compared (Rapson, page CVII) with the rev. type "Discus, Bow and Arrow" of certain copper coins struck conjointly by Spalirisez and Azes (Percy Gardner, B. M. cat., Greek and Scythic kings, Pl. XXII., 4; C. Nehr, 1890, Pl. VII, 13). On the other hand, the insignia Lion capital and Dharmachakra were those of the Kshaharâtas of Mathurâ; and in particular the Lion pillar of Mathurâ is well known. We know that the Pahlava Spalirises and the Śaka Azes were kings of Arachosia and Sistân. Azes I reigned in the Panjâb and it would not be impossible that he founded the Vikrama era which begins in 58 B. C. "........he (Azes I) was reigning in the third quarter "of the first century B. C., while the probability that he may "have founded an era is also suggested by the abundance of "his coins, which denote his pre-eminence among the Śaka-

"Pahlava sovereigns" (J. R. A. S. for 1914, page 177—" The date of Kaṇishka" by J. H. Marshall). We may therefore place the reign of Bhûmaka approximately in the second quarter of the first century B. C. (50 to 25 B. C.)

The coins bearing the name "Nahapâna" that were rare at one time have become abundant since the discovery of a treasure containing 13250 coins at Joghaltembhi, near Nâsik (see J. B. B. R. A. S. Vol. XXII, Art. XVI, page 223). This discovery has made a complete study of it possible. It must first be noted that this coinage extends over a very long period of time. It is not possible to give the exact number of years but it is certainly very large. In fact, we may observe very clearly a certain "evolution" in the style of the coins. For instance, these coins contain two legends one in Greek and the other in Kharoshṭhî, but these two writings evolve inversely: when the legend in Kharoshṭhî is very legible, that in Greek is debased, and on the coins in which the Kharoshṭhi legend is debased the Greek legend is visible. Such an evolution can be produced only during a very large number of years. We know that with the lapse of time, Kharoshṭhî disappeared, little by little, from the coinage of India. (see J. R. A. S. for 1904, page 373.) Here I have to make another important remark. These coins bear an effigy which surely is not that of a single individual, since the nose is sometimes aquiline and sometimes straight. Further, the most ancient coins represent sometimes a young man, and sometimes an old man, as is the case also with the less ancient coins. "The Rev. H. R. Scott has pointed out that they exhibit an extraordinary diversity, not only in apparent age but also in features. They cannot possibly have been portraits, in the true sense of the word of, any single individual" (Rapson, page CX). What conclusions are we to draw from these remarks ? We cannot say it exactly. It is possible that many kings called "Nahapâna" have reigned in succession. But we may also suppose that there were only one or two Nahapânas, but that, after them, they have continued to use their coinage for a long time. The latter hypothesis will explain the extraordinary diversity in the effigies ; the most ancient coins bear the image of the Nahapâna that reigned at this epoch and the less ancient ones contain the image of some figure made to vary according to the fancy of the coiner.

The coins struck in the name of Nahapàna resemble much those of king Ràjùvula (see the plate facing the page 630 of J. R. A. S. for 1913). This is quite natural as Nahapâna and Ràjùvula both belong to the Kshaharâta dynasty. But there is an epigraphical detail which proves well the relationship that exists between the coinages of the two branches of this very Kshaharàta dynasty: "........ the letter H found on a coin of Kharahostes and on some of those of Nahapâna......" (J. R. A. S., 1913, page 1013). Concerning the origin of this letter H we shall be content with giving here the opinion of Mr. Thomas (J. R. A. S., 1913, page 1013, note): " I think this H to be not Roman, but Aramaic (it is no accident that it is found only on Śaka-Pahlava coins)".

The coins bearing the name of Nahapâna contain the insignia "thunderbolt" and "arrow". Mr. Vincent A. Smith has written ("Early History of India," 3rd. Edition, page 218): "The arrow and thunderbolt of Nahapâna's coins connect him with the Parthians and the Northern Satraps Hagâna and Hagâmâsha (see Cat. coins in I. M., Vol. I., page 195)". And Nahapâna is a good old Persian name (J. R. A. S. for 1906, p. 211, No. 17.)

A Kshaharâta king named Nahapâna is found mentioned in several inscriptions engraved on the rock-cut excavations in Mahârâshṭra, viz. at Kàrli, Nâsik and Junnar. These inscriptions say that the daugther of Nahapâna named Dakshamitrà, married a Śaka (Ep. Ind, Vol. VIII, p. 85) called Ushavadâta (Rishabadatta) son of Dinika (inscriptions Nos. 1132 and 1134 of Lüders's list.) This princess and her husband made numerous gifts to the Buddhist monks and had many roc-cut monasteries dug for them. Some of these grants were made at Pokhara (Ajmer) and at Ujêni (Ujjain) which proves that the dominion of Nahapâna extended over an immense empire comprising Guzarât (Kutch, Surâshṭra, etc.), a part of Ràjputànà, Màḷwâ (Ujjain) and all the northwestern part of the Deccan (Mahârâshṭra).

We may often estimate the greatness of empires by the beauty of their monuments. It is therefore probable that the reign of Nahapâna was very glorious, as some of the monuments constructed during his reign are among the most splendid in India. One of these is the Buddhist temple cut in the rock at Kârlî, the immense nave of which equals in grandeur that of the Gothic churches. It is noteworthy that the monuments containing the inscriptions of Nahapâna (at Junnar, Kârlî, Nâsik) are all in the same style. This style resembles much that of the balustrade of the grand stûpa at Sâñchi. We have already said that this balustrade was probably begun between 70 B. C. and 60 B. C. It must certainly have taken a sufficiently long time to build, for, the style of the sculptures shows that the gateways may be arranged chronologically in the folowing order: (1) Southern, (2) Northern, (3) Eastern (4) Western, (Archæological Survey of India; Report for 1913-14, page 9.) It is therefore probable that most of the sculptures of Sâñchi date from 50. B. C. to I. A. D. and that the monuments containing the inscriptions of Nahapâna have been sculptured shortly before the beginning of our era.

Many of these inscriptions are dated; we have at Nâsik (No. 1133 of Lüders's list) the years 41, 42 and 45. At Junnar an inscription (No. 1174 of Lüders's list) that records a grant of Ayama (Aryaman), minister of Nahapâna, give us the date 46. A reign of 46 years is rare; we may therefore suppose that these 46 years are not counted from the year of the coronation of Nahapâna but from the beginning of a particular era. This supposition seems to be confirmed by some other documents. We know that the satraps of Mathurâ belonged to the dynasty of Kshaharâtas and that one of them Râjûvula (Ranjubula) struck coins similar to those of Nahapâna, and we may suppose that they were contemporaries. The son of this Râjûvula named Śoḍâsa has left an inscription in Mathurâ (No. 59 of Lüders's list) dated in the year 72 [Âmohinî record]. Here there can be no doubt. Here it is question of the year 72 of a particular era, for, it is improbable that Śoḍâsa reigned 72 years. Moreover, Mr. Devadatta Ramkrishna Bhandarkar has affirmed (page 275, Vol. XX of Vol. XX of the Journal of the Bombay branch of the Royal Asiatic Society) "I maintain that on similar palæographic grounds Nahapâna must be supposed to be prior to Śôḍâsa" and we find a complete justification of this opinion in his paper ('A Kushan stone inscription'). Thus Palæography proves that the inscriptions of Nahapâna which are dated 41, 42, 45, 46, are more archaic than the inscription of Śoḍâsa which is dated in the year 72. As these two princes belong to the same family of Kshaharâtas (J. R. A. S. for 1912 p. 122) and the coinage of Nahapâna resembles that of Râjûvula, father of Śôḍâsa, it is natural to suppose that Nahapâna and Sôḍâsa dated their inscriptions from the same era. What can this era be? It is generally admitted now that the inscription of Śoḍâsa is dated from the Vikrama era which begins in 58 B. C. If, then, the Vikrama era was no other than the Kshaharâta era, the inscriptions of Nahapâna at Nâsik and Junar will be dated in the years 17, 16, 13 and 12. B. C. These dates perfectly agree with the facts furnished by archæology. We have said that the art of the monuments of Nahapâna at Kârli and Nâsik resemble fhat of the grand Śtûpa at Sâñchi. It must be noted now that the art of the monuments of Nahapâna differs much from the art of the epoch of Kaṇishka. The discovery of the casket in which Kaṇishka locked up the relies of Buddha has proved, that in the time of Kaṇishka, Buddha was represented with the head adorned with an aureole and the body dressed in a robe with long folds. It is thus that Buddha is very often represented at Amarâvati. We see nothing like it in the monuments of Nahapâna. It will be too long to give here a detailed history of the evolution of the Hindu art; we shall content ourselves with saying that we can approximately determine the age of the sculptures from the ornamentation and the style. We think it is useless to take up this question again, since we have already developed this theory at great length in Vol. I of our work, "Archæologie du Sud de l'Inde" ,Vol. I, Architecture. In the course of a series of tours that I made in the Deccan in 1910 - 11, I collected photographs of the principal monuments in this region and particularly those of Kârli and Nâsik. Illustrations intended to support the theory developed in chapters I & II, (pages 15 to 49) of the book will be found in plates I to IX. That theory is the following: there is a difference between the monuments that are anterior to the Christian era and those that are posterior to it. The monuments of Nahapâna at Nâsik and Kârli are of the same family as the stúpa at Sâñchi and are anterior to Jesus-Christ. On the contrary, the sculptures of the epoch of Kaṇishka, those of the tope at Amarâvatî, the caves of Gautamiputra at Nâsik and of Yajña Śri at Kaṇhêri are posterior to Jesus-Christ and are characterised by a very particular kind of ornamentation.

In short, the coinage, palœography and the style of the monuments prove, that, at the beginning of the Christian era there reigned on the shores of the Gulf of Cambay one or more princes bearing the name of Nahapâna. A Nahapâna who had Ushavadâta for his son-in-law reigned in the years 41, 42, 45 and 46 of an unknown era. There reigned in Mathurâ some princes of the same dynasty of Kshaharâtas, These princes were: Hagâna, Hagâmâsha, Râjûvula, Śoḍâsa Kharahostes and Kalni, and they used a special era. If it is admitted that it is the Vikrama era (58 B. C.) we find that Śoḍasâ reigned in 14 or 15 A. D. which well coincides with the information furnished by archæology (it is the opinion of the Director-general of Archæology, Mr. J. H. Marshall, see J. R. A. S. for 1914, page 986). The coins show that Nahapâna was very nearly the contemporary of Hagâna and Hagâmàsha and so it will be a little before the beginning of the Christian era. This is in perfect accord with the supposition that the inscriptions of Nahapâna are dated from the Vikrama era. However, "the question has not been settled" (Vincent A. Smith, the Oxford History of India, 1919, page 153, footnote 1).

Who succeeded Nahapâna or the Nahapânas? It is probable that about the year 20 A. D., Gondopharnes, king of the Panjâb, became master of a great empire that extended all over the west of India; he conquered Arachosia, Sind and the country near the mouth of the Indus; the successors of Nahapâna were probably simple governors of provinces. On the death of Gondophares this empire was parcelled out into petty principalities. The Panjàb fell into the hands of his nephew Abdagases; Arachosia and Sind passed under the rule of Orthagnes who was followed by Pakorês [concerning Orthagnes, see Gardner, page 109, Pl. XXIII, 9; concerning Pacores, see gardner, page 110, Pl. XXIII, 8]

The "Periplus of the Erythraean Sea" gives a description

of this region at it was at that timê. The date of this work has been determined recently by Mr. J. Kennedy (J. R. A. S. for 1918, page 106). The Periplus mentions Malichas who lived in 67 A. D. and died in 71 A. D. It is therefore probable that the anonymous author of Periplus went on his travels about the year 70 A. D. The Periplus gives a description of the valley of the Lower Indus, which he called Skythia "which is governed, however, by Parthian princes, who are perpetually at strife among themselves expelling each other" (Periplus, Ind. Ant. Vol. VIII, page 138). This description applies perfectly well to the state of Sind after Gondophares. The Periplus mentions two princes of the northern part of the Deccan : the king of Barygaza (Bharukacha=Broach) whose name ends in "*bares*" (Kennedy, J. R. A. S. for 1918, pages 108 and 113—"Nambanos-Nahapāna is a myth") and the king of Kalliena (Kalyan) who was called Sandanes who was hostile to the foreigners.

Cave No. 3 at Nâsik contains an inscriptions (insc. No. 2.—see Ep. Ind. Vol. VIII, page 61, and Lüders's list No. 1123) which is well-known for the information that it gives. We learn that the king Gautamîputra Sri Śâtakarṇi "destroyed the Śakas, Yavanas, Palhavas, rooted out the Kshaharâta race and restored the Śâtavâhana family."

The inscription says further that Gautamiputra Śri Śâtakarṇi was king of the following countries : Asika, Asaka, Muḷaka, Suraṭha, Kukura, Aparanta, Anupa, Vidarbha, Âkarâvanti. Since these countries once formed part of the kingdom of the Kshaharâtas, we may conclude that Śâtakarṇi took possession of them after the destruction of the Kshaharâtas (Suraṭha=Surâshṭra=Kâthiâwâṛ; Âkaravanti=Mâlwâ; Aparanta=the region along the coast, north of Bombay.)

The destruction of the Kshaharatas by Gautamiputra is fully confirmed by the coinage; in fact, out of 13250 coins bearing the name of Nahapâna that were discovered at Joghaltembhi, there are 9270 that have been re-struck by Gautamiputra. The re-striking of the Kshaharâta coins by Gautamiputra is for us a very valuable information, for, we may then know for certain what kind of coinage the Śâtavâhanas had at the time of the destruction of the Śakas. The obverse bears the "Ujjain symbol" and the reverse the symbol "chaitya".

From the fact that all the coin re-struck by Gautamîputra bear the name "Nahapâna", certain authors have come to the conclusion that it was Ushavâdata own father-in-law that was vanquished: "Gautamiputra ktlled Nahapâna". A closer examination of the coins proves exactly the contrary. Rev. H. R. Scott has made three observations: (1) that the coinage bearing the name of Nahapâna extend over a very long period, since it had had the time to evolve considerably. (2) The effigies are of "extraordinary diversity" and "cannot possibly have been portraits, in the true sense of the word of any single individual" (Rapson, page CX). The-first two remarks show that, very probably, the coins bearing the name of Nahapâna have not *all of them* come from the Nahapâna of the inscriptions so the coins containing the name of Nahapâna cannot allow us to draw any conclusion concerning the Nahapâna of the inscriptions. But the third remark is still more important. (3) "Judging from the condition of the coins, I should say that they must have been a very long time in circulation.........before.........being counter struck" (J. B.1B. R. A. S. Vol. XXII, page 224). The last remark shows that, *even if* we admit that the Nahapâna of the inscriptions has issued *the most recent* coins of the whole group, "a very long time" must have elapsed between him and Gautamiputra. That is the opinion of Mr. Vincent A. Smith (Early History of India, 3rd Edition, 1914, page 217): "It is not necessary to believe that Gautamîputra Ândhra fought with Nahapânâ personally. Study of the great Joghaltembhi hoard of more than 13000 coins of Nahapâna proves that the coinage extended over many years, although always bearing the name of Nahapâna, who I believe was dead before Gautamipuira extirpated his family or clan". Bühler and Bhagwanlal believed that they could read in one of the Nâsik inscriptions that Gautamiputra made a gift of a field belonging "till to-day" (till then) to Ushavadâta. But M. Sénart (Ep. Ind. Vol. VIII, page 72) has proved that the word "ajakâlikiyam" means quite a different thing. Besides, the omission of Nahapâna's name in mentioning the destruction of the Kshaharâtas in the Nâsik inscription proves that Gautamîputra has not encountred this great king. All the inscriptions of Ushavadâta are in too archaic an alphabet for us to suppose that he was the contemporary of Gautamîputra. Again, in my work "Archéologie du Sud de l'Inde" Vol. I., I have shown by figure 19 (Vihâras of Nâsik) that the style of Nahapâna differs much from that of Gautamiputra; and *these differences are due to time*, since there is *evolution* of architecture [for instance the "bell-shaped" capitals have been replaced by the "pot shaped" ones. This transformation of the form of a bell into that of a sphere has needed at least one century]. Thus then, architecture and palæography perfectly agree with the coinage to prove that "a very long time" has elapsed between the Nahapâna of the inscriptions, and Gautamiputra, the destroyer of the Śakas.

§ 2. Chashṭana, founder of the Śaka era.

During three centuries, Ujjain was the capital of a dynasty of kings whose genealogy begins thus:—

Chashṭana
|
Jayadâman
|
Rudradâman
|
Dâmajadaśri
|
Jîvadâman.

There is no room for doubting that Rudradâman, the representative of the third generation reigned in 130 A. D. Indeed, in 1905-06, Professor Dêvadatta Ramkṛishṇa Bhandarkar (Archæol. Survey Western India-Progress Report for 1905-06, page 35) has made very important discovery of several inscriptions of Rudradâman dated in the 52nd year of an era which is incontestably (see J. R. A. S. 1899, page 365) the Śaka era (78 A. D); they are the inscriptions of Andhau in Cutch.

The text of the inscription is as follows: Râjña Châshṭanasa Ysâmotikaputrasa râjña Rudradâmasa Jayadâmaputrasa varshe dvipachâśe 50, 2. (Progress Report, Archæol. Survey of India; Western Circle 1914-1915, 67).

As the same text is reproduced in many inscriptions, it must be considered correct and there is no room to think that a fragment of it has either been lost or accidentally omitted by the engraver. Since we know from various documents that Jayadâman was the son of Châshṭana, the meaning of this text is certainly the following: "In the 52nd year, in the reign of Rudradâman, son of Jayadâman, grandson of Châshṭana and great-grandson of Ysâmotika". This meaning has been accepted for the last 15 years. Very recently, however, Professor Devadatta Ramkrishna Bhandarkar (Dekkan of the Śâtavâhana period, Ind. Ant., Vol. XLVII, part DXCVI., June 1918, page 154, footnote 26) has proposed a new interpretation. According to him the inscriptions will be dated in the common reign of Chashṭana and Rudradâman who would have reigned conjointly: "at first, I was inclined "to supply "pautrasa" after Ysâmotikaputrasa and refer the "date to the reign of Rudradâman (J. B. B. R. A. S., Vol. "XXIII., page 68) Mr. R. C. Majumdar of the Calcutta "University has kindly offered the suggestion that the date "has better be referred to the conjoint reign of Chashṭana and "Rudradâman". This interpretation is not possible: if here it was question of common reign of Chashṭana *and* Rudradâman, the text would be "Rudradâmasa *cha* varshe" or something else which will show that it was the reign of two persons; but here there is no possibility of any doubt; "Râjña Rudradâmasa Jayadâmaputrasa varshe" can mean only one thing: "the reign of Rudradâman". The inscriptions of Andhau are therefore dated in the reign of Rudradâman and in the 52nd year of the Śaka era which corresponds to 130 A. D.

We know (see Rapson, page CXXIV), that Jivadâman, the representative of the fifth generation, reigned (as Mahâkshatrapa) in Śaka 100 which corresponds to 180 A. D. We may suppose that this king ascended the throne about 2 years before it, in 178 A. D. and we may attribute a reign of 23 years to his father Dâmajadaśri. We thus obtain the following chronology:—

Dâmajadaśri, acc. circ. 155 A. D.,

|

Jivadâman, acc. circ. 178 A. D.

I request the reader to note that this chronology is not something imagined by me: if we open the book of Mr. Vincent A. Smith "Early History of India" 3rd edition, we shall find a plate facing page 218, giving the chronology of Western Kshatrapas; and we shall find there the same dates: Dâmajadaśri, acc. circ. 155 A. D.—Jivadaman, acc. circ. 178 A. D. I have therefore adopted the opinion of Mr. Vincent A. Smith which is certainly very near the truth.

We know the coins of Jayadâman as Kshatrapa, but coins

of this prince bearing the title of Mahâkshatrapa have not been discovered so far. If therefore we admit that Jayadâman did not reign at all or reigned only for a short time, we can conclude therefrom that the reign of his father Chashṭana and his son Rudradàman have been long. But what is the duration of a long reign?

In the history of the Pallavas there is the example of king Nandivarman Pallavamalla who reigned for more than 62 years (Tâṇḍantôttâm plates, 58th year and Tiruvallam insc. No. 76 of 1889, 62nd year) and was succeeded by his son Dantivarman who reigned for more than 51 years (Tiruchchâṇûr insc. No. 262 of 1904, 51st. year). But such instances are rare and we shall admit that a reign of average length is one of 25 to 30 years and that a long reign may last from 35 to 40 years. So, if we allow that Jayadâman did not reign at all or reigned only a very short time and that the reigns of Rudradâman and Chashṭana were long, we get the following chronology:—

Chashṭana, acc. circ. 75 or 85 A. D.

Jayadâman (was living circ. 110 or 115 A. D)

Rudradâman, acc. circ 115 or 120 A. D

Dâmajadaśri, acc. circ. 155 A. D.

The only objection that has been made to the above chronology is the folowing: "The inscriptions of Nahapâna are dated in the Śaka era."

It is certain that Chashṭana ascended the throne after the destruction of the Kshaharâtas; an examination of the coins proves it (see Rapson, page 72, Pl. X). When Chasṭana bore only the title of Kshatrapa (var. b; Pl. x: El and No. 259) and later on assumed the title of Mahâkshatrapa (Rapson, Pl. X., No. 260 and ff.) we find on the reverse of his coins the symbol "chaitya with three arches" identically the same as that of the coins restruck by Gautamiputra. The symbol "Chaitya with three arches" on the coins of Chashṭana proves incontestably that Chashṭana was a Satrap of Gautamîputra after the destruction of the Kshaharâtas.

If then the inscriptions of Nahapâna which bear the dates 41, 42, 45 and 46 are dated from the Śaka era and correspond to 119, 120, 123 and 124 A. D. we must admit that Chashṭana ascended the throne after 124 A. D.

This supposition clashes with difficulties which have been exposed by Mr. Rakhal Das Banerji in a paper entitled "Nahapâna and the Śaka era" in the "Journal of the Royal Asiatic Society" for 1917, page 273.

We know that Chashṭana reigned first as a Kshatrapa and afterwards as a Mahâkshatrapa. We have the coins of Jayadâman only as Kshatrapa. So, these coins bear the "Chaitya with six arches" instead of the "Chaitya with three arches" which seems to show that Jayadâman reigned as a Kshatrapa for a sufficiently long time after the destruction of the Kshaharâtas. (Rapson, page 76, No. 265 to 268). But, if we admit that the inscriptions of Nahapâna are dated in the Śaka era, there will be only an interval of five years between the inscription of this king dated 46 and the inscriptions of Rudradâman dated 52. Within these years (years 47, 48, 49, 50 and 51), must have taken place :

(1) The end of Nahapâna' s reign ;

(2) The destruction of the Kshaharâtas;

(3) The accession of Chashṭana as Kshatrapa, his reign as Kshatrapa, his accession as a Mahâkshatrapa, and his reign as Mahâkshatrapa ;

(4) The accession of Jayadâman as Kshatrapa, his reign as Kshatrapa, and perhaps also his reign as Mahâkshatrapa ;

(5) The accession of Rudradâman and the beginning of his reign.

That all these events took place within five years, *it is not impossible, but it is not probable.* It is not probable that the Kshaharâtas were destroyed *soon* after the inscription at Junnar; it is not probable that the reigns of Chashṭana, first as Kshatrapa then as Mahâkshatrapa and of Jayadâman as Kshatrapa and perhaps also as Mahâkshatrapa have taken only four or five years ; and it is not probable that Rudradâman ascended the throne exactly before Andhau inscriptions were engraved.

A rash guesser may be allowed to suppose that Rudradâman ascended the throne only four or five years after the end of the reign of Nahapâna, But for laying down such a supposition he must entirely disregard all information obtained from the archæology, numismatics, palaeography and philology of India.

(a) Archæology shows us that the architectural style, the ornamental design and the costumes of the personages of the epoch of Nahapâna clearly point to an archaic epoch very near the beginning of the Christian era and that it is impossible to place Nahapâna in the 2nd century A. D;

(b) Numismatics shows that Nahapâna was the contemporary of the Satraps, Hagâna and Hagâmâsha, that the coins of Nahapâna were in circulation for a very long time and a still long period elapsed before they were restruck by Gautamiputra;

(c) Palæography shows that the alphabet of the inscriptions of Nahapâna is more archaic than that of Śoḍâsa and much more archaic than that of Rudradâman. To say that the inscriptions of Nahapâna are almost contemporaneous with those of Rudradâman and that there was only a five years' interval between the reigns of these two kings is to introduce a monstrous anachronism into the palæography of these inscriptions;

(d) Comparative philology shows that all the inscriptions of Nahapâna are in Prâkṛit whereas all the inscriptions of Rudradâman are in Sanskṛit.

Upon the whole, we are not sure of the epoch of Nahapâna, but we are quite sure that the inscriptions of Nahapâna are not dated in the Śaka era ; and nothing prevents us from admitting that Chashṭana ascended the throne between 75 and 85 A. D.

But, then, can Chashṭana be the founder of the Śaka era, since the 1st year of this era corresponds to 79 A. D ?

Some persons will say: "No, Chashṭana has not founded the Śaka era, because it was Kaṇishka that founded it." It is therefore necessary to take up the question of the date of Kaṇishka.

This question is perhaps one that has been very hotly discussed and though it is not yet completely settled, it is much more clear today than it was 10 years ago. After the skilful excavations of Mr. J. H. Marshall (see J. R. A. S.; 1914, pages 973-86; and 1915, pages 991-16), it is not possible any more to place Kaṇishka before the two Kadphisês.

Besides, the close resemblance existing between the coins of Kadphisês I. and those of Augustus and Tiberius does not allow any doubt in regard to the approximate age of Kujula-Kadphisês. As Fleet says : "We do not dispute in any way the view that at some time closely about A. D. 50, the sovereignty in the Kabul territory passed from the Greek king Hermaeus to the Kushan prince Kozoulo-Kadphisês, whose son Wêmo-Kadphisês then established a Kushan empire in Northern India" (J. R. A. S., 1913, p. 969).

We may therefore say now that it is certain that Kaṇishka did not come to the throne before about 75 A. D.

This date marks the earliest limit, but Kaṇishka might have ascended the throne much later. Very recently, a scholar (Ind. Ant, Vol. XLVI.—Part DLXXXVIII, page 261) thought that he had proved that the era founded by Kaṇishka was the Kaḷachuri era of 248 A. D. This is not possible. In fact, the reign of Vâsudêva, the last of the Kushâns, came to an end 100 years after the beginning of the reign of Kaṇishka. Numerous inscriptions prove that Vâsudêva reigned at Mathurâ. It is certain that this country over which extended the empire of Vâsudêva was occupied about 350 A. D. by the Yaudhêyas and the Nâgas and it is probable that they reigned in this place nearly one century before they were subjugated by Samudra-Gupta. The capitals of the Nâgas were Mathurâ, Kântipura and Padmâvati (or Pawêya, at the confluence of the Sindhu and the Para). We know the name of Śivanaṁdi (Archæological Survey of India, for 1915-1916) who was a predecessor of Gaṇapati Nâga the rival of Samudra-Gupta. We have also coins of Gaṇapatinâga (Bühler's Grundriss, Ind. coins § 101, Pl. V, 2). Nâgasêna, heir of the house of Padmâvati, mentioned in Harsha-charita (page 221), (see J. R. A. S. for 1899, page 448), has been identified by Mr. E. J. Rapson with the Nâgasêna of the pillar at Allâhâbâd. We know also the coins (Ind. coins, § 101) of Prabhâkara (J. R. A. S. for 1900, page 117), of Skandanâga, of Devanâga (Cunningham, coins of Mediæval India, pp. 23 and 24) and of Bhîmanâga (Progress Report Arch. Surv. Western Circle for 1914-15, page 60).

The Yaudhêyas were formidable at the time of Rudradâman; but the Girnar inscription tells us that they were vanquished probably shortly before the year 150 A. D. It is probably after the death of Vâsudêva that they established themselves in the Mathurâ region. We have a stone inscription (Gupta Inscriptions, No. 58, Plate XXXVI, B) found at Bijayagadh [or Bêjêgaḍh, about two miles to the South West of Byânâ, the chief town of the Byânâ tahsil of the Bharatpur (Bhurtpoor) state in Ràjputânâ] which has come to us from the Yaudhêyas and which enables us to know the geographical position of their empire. The alphabet of the inscriptions is intermediate between that of the last Kushâns and that of the first Guptas. We have also the coins of this dynasty (Cunningham, Coins of Anc. Ind. Pl. VI., 6-8); and the Yaudhêyas are mentioned in line 22 of the inscription on the pillar at Allâhâbâd (No. 1 of Gupta Inscriptions). The invasion of Samudra-Gupta took place in the middle of the IV century. If we take nearly one century as the duration of the reigns of the Yaudhêyas and the Nâgas, we find that Vâsudêva ceased to reign before about 250 A. D. and that Kaṇishka came to the throne before about 150 A. D.

So the accession of Kaṇishka should be placed between 75 A. D. and 150 A. D.

We know that Kaṇishka founded an era and we have just seen that he came to the throne between 75 and 150 A. D. Can Kaṇishka be the founder of the Śaka era which begins at the end of 78 A. D.? I believe that this hypothesis is not probable for the following reasons:

(1) If we admit that Kujula-Kadphisês and Hermœus reigned about 50 A. D. and that Kaṇishka founded the Śaka era in 78 A. D., we have scarcely 28 years for the duration of the end of the reign of Vima-Kadphisês (I) and the whole of the reign of Kujula-Kadphisês (II). It is probable that Kadphisês I. reigned long and died when he was about 80 years old. Secondly, the reign of Kadphisês (II) was probably very long (at least 40 years); that is the opinion of Mr. Vincent A. Smith: "No definite proof of the length of his reign can " given, but the extent of the conquests made by Kadphisês " II. and the large volume of his coinage are certain indi- " cations that his reign was protracted. Cunningham " assigned it a duration of forty years." (Early History of India, 2nd Ed. page 239, foot note 1).

Again, it is not certain that Kaṇishka was the immediate successor of Kadphisês II.

So, it is not possible that Kaṇishka should have come to the throne in 79 A. D.

(2) We do not know exactly in what era are dated the inscription of the year 103 of Gondophares and the inscriptions of the years 113 and 122 of the Kushâns ; if we suppose that it is the Vikrama era, the dates agree so well with all the information furnished by history, palæography, and the coins, that most of the savants have accepted this hypothesis. For example, the year 103 of this era being the 26th year of Gondophares, he must have come to the throne in 19 A. D. And Gondophares uses the title "autocrator" which was introduced by Augustus and adopted by the Parthian king Phraates IV (8 to 11 A. D.). Mr. Marshall has discovered at Taxila (J. R. A. S., for 1914, pp. 973, 978) in the "Chir Stûpa" a document dated 136, which, in the Vikrama era, corresponds to 79 A. D., and the king mentioned therein is probably Kadphisês I, but certainly not Kaṇishka (see "Taxila insc. of year 136" by Sten Konow, in Ep. Ind. Vol. XIV., pp. 284 to 288). This discovery is enough to shake the conviction of those that attribute to Kaṇishka the era of 78 A. D.

(3) Mr. Sten Konow has shown recently (Ep. Ind., Vol. XIV., pages 141 and 290) that the Tibetan and Chinese documents tend to prove that Kaṇishka reigned in the 2nd century and not in the 1st.

(4) The scholars who thought that Kaṇishka founded the era 78 A. D. believed also that he introduced in India the Græco-Buddhistic art in all its splendour. But when the reliquary bearing an inscription of Kaṇishka was discovered, one might expect that this work of art chiselled under the pious orders of the great king would be a splendid work of Greek art. Alas ! The sculptures are deplorably inferior in workmanship and undoubtedly represent an art in full decadence. A further attentive study of the art of Kaṇishka has shown that this king did not reign certainly in the Ist century.

(5) Mr. Sten Konow has shown recently (Ep. Ind. Vol. XIV., page. 141) that the inscriptions of the Kaṇishka era and those of the Śaka era are not dated in the same fashion : "It " becomes impossible to maintain that Kaṇishka was the founder

4

" of the Śaka era and used it in his inscriptions because then
" it becomes unintelligible why he should have changed the
" way of expressing the dates".

We shall therefore conclude that Kaṇishka is not the founder of the Śaka era.

The preceding lines had already been written when I had the honour of receiving from Mr. Vincent A. Smith a copy of "The Oxford History of India," Oxford, 1919, and I read in page 127 : "It may now be affirmed with confidence that the " order of the five leading Kushân kings is finally settled, and " that the uncertainty as to the chronology has been reduced " to a period of forty years in round numbers or to state it " otherwise, the question is, "Did Kaṇishka come to the " throne in A. D. 78, or about forty years later ?". When the " third edition of the "Early History of India" was published " in 1914, my narrative was based upon the working hypothesis " that Kaṇishka's accession took place in A. D. 78, although " it was admitted to be possible that the true date might be " later. Further consideration of the evidence from Taxila " now available leads me to follow Sir John Marshall and " Professor Sten Konow in dating the beginning of Kaṇishka's " reign approximatively in A. D. 120, a date which I had " advocated many years ago on different grounds".

Since the Śaka era was not founded either by Nahapâna or by Kaṇishka and as Gautamîputra also was not the founder of it (no one has made this supposition), there remain but two hypotheses : that the Śaka era was founded either by Chashṭana or by Kadphisês II. The latter opinion is held by Dr. Sten Konow who has written recently "I am still of opinion that the Śaka era was established by Vima-Kadphisês". (The Ara inscription, in Ep. Ind. Vol. XIV., p. 141).

For such a theory to be *possible*, Kadphisês II must have reiged in 78-79 A. D. We may believe that the inscription of the "Chir Stûpa" at Taxila is dated in the 136th year of the era which begins in 58-57 B. C. and the date 136 falls precisely in 78-79 A. D. And if we study the inscription of the "Chir Stûpa" and ask ourselves who is the king therein mentioned, we are rather inclined to reply: "It is an inscription of Kujula-Kadphisês (I)" : "So far as I can see, there cannot be much doubt that the Kushaṇa Emperor of the Panjtâr and Taxila records was Kujula-Kadphisês and not Vima-Kadphisês" (Ep. Ind. Vol. XIV Part VII, July 1918, page 289. "Taxila inscription of the year 136" by Sten Konow). It is not therefore probable that (Vima) Kadphisês II reigned in 78-79 A. D.

But even granting that Kadphisês II. reigned in 78-79 A. D. it has to be proved that he founded an era. We have not even a single document that can make us believe that Kadphisês II has founded an era. On the contrary, if the "Chir Stûpa" inscription is dated 78-79 A. D., it will be proved that the Kushân Kings used after A. D. 78 the era 58-57 B. C.; and finally, granting that Kadphisês II. founded an era, it must be proved that this era was adopted by Chashṭana or his descendants.

After all, the theory of (Vima) Kadphisês II having founded the Śaka era is not based either upon any proof or even indication.

There remains then but one hypothesis : "The Śaka era was founded by Chashṭana". This theory was expressed 30 years ago by Cunningham (see N. chr. 1888, p. 232 and 1892, p. 44) discussed notably by D. R. Bhandarkar (B. B. R. A. S., Vol., XX page 280) and was afterwards completely abandoned.

I now wish to assert boldly that this abandonment is quite unjustified. This theory has been slighted because for 30 years the historians of India have had two preconceived notions : (1) that the inscriptions of Nahapâna are dated in the Śaka era. (2) that the Śaka era was founded by Kaṇishka. I think I have proved that these two suppositions are now untenable.

I affirm that the only natural theory concerning the Śaka era is that it was founded by Chashṭana.

It is admitted on all hands that the dynasty of Chashṭana has used the Śaka era; and it is but *natural* to suppose that the founder of the dynasty was also the founder of the era used by it. Outside the kingdom of Chashṭana and his descendants, not a single inscription has been found which is dated in the above era. In fact the inscriptions of the Kushân kings are not dated from the Śaka era and the inscriptions dated from the same era which are found in South India are all posterior to the fall of the dynasty of Chashṭana. Thus then all the Śaka inscriptions that are anterior to 400 A. D. are every one of them inscriptions of the dynasty of Chashṭana. The era is therefore special to that dynasty.

If we are not quite sure that Chashṭana was a Śaka, there is no doubt that he was of foreign origin. The names of the members of this family show that they were foreigners. Mr. Rapson says (page CXXI) : "Ghsamotika is Scythic"; "shṭana (in Châshṭana) is a Persian termination "; and (page CXXII) Dâmaghsada "foreign name, may possibly be an attempt to express the Persian Zâda, a son".

A general of the W. Kshatrapas is mentioned in an inscription (Progress Report, Arch. Survey, Western India for 1917-1918, page 37) as being a Śaka.

Were Chashṭana and his descendants themselves Śakas ? It is possible; but one thing is certain, that in ancient India they were designated by the name of Śakas. The Matsya Purâna mentions a dynasty of 18 Śakas which is probably that of Chashṭana; but there can be no doubt in certain cases : for instance, Bâna in circ. 630 A. D. has written ("Harsha charita" trans. Cowell and Thomas, page 194) : "In his enemy's city, the king of the Śakas, while courting another man's wife, was butchered by Chandra-Gupta".

To sum up :

(1) It is certain that all the dates that are given in the documents of the dynasty of Chashṭana are of the Śaka era.

(2) We do not know of even a single inscription anterior to 400 A. D. which is dated in the Śaka era and belongs to a dynasty other than that of Chashṭana.

(3) Tradition has given the name of Śaka to the era beginning in 78 A. D., since it was the era used by the descendants of Chahṭana who in ancient India were designated by the name of "Śaka."

(4) The most ancient inscriptions (Andhau) are dated in the year 52 of this era; and they are the inscriptions of the grandson of the founder of the dynasty. If the founder of the dynasty was also the founder of the era, it is quite natural that the grandson should have reigned 52 years later.

Therefore, the most simple, the most natural and the most logical theory consists in saying : "The Śaka era of 78 was founded by Chashṭana".

§ 3. The later Śâtavâhana kings.

If 79 A. D. is the first year of the reign of Chashṭana, it is probable that the destruction of the Kshaharâtas by Gautamiputra took place in 78 A. D. or a little earlier.

It is probable that Chashṭana was a Śaka prince, who, for some reasons not known, entered into an alliance with Gautamîputra against the Kshaharâtas. Perhaps he was either a petty prince of Sind or Râjputâna who invaded the Kshaharâta empire or a vassal of the Kshaharâtas who revolted against his suzerain.

The fòrm of the hair on the head of Chashṭana differs from that of the king represented on the coins bearing the name of Nabapâna.

It seems that Chashṭana was first a vassal of Gautamiputra for the following three reasons : (1) Chashṭana first bore only the title of Kshatrapa (2) The reverse side of the coins of Chashṭana contains the Chaitya with 3 arches which characterises the coins restruck by Gautamiputra (3) The Nâsik inscription says that Gautamîputra was the lord of Surâshṭra and Mâḷwâ.

However, Chashṭana, even as a Kshatrapa, had coins struck in his own name, and there is room to think that the powers of Gautamîputra in the states of Chashṭana were only nominal.

The mother of Gautamiputra was the queen Gautami Balaśri which justifies the name of Gautamiputra borne by her son. We know, in fact, that the kings of this epoch often added before their name the gòtra of their mother.

The son of Gautamîputra reigned under the name of Vâsishṭhiputra Śrî Puḷumâvi.

The famous Nâsik inscription, in which the queen Balaśrî, mother of Gautamîputra and grandmòther of Vâsishṭhiputra Pulumâvi, tells us that her son destroyed the Śakas, is dated in the 19th year of the reign of her grandson Puḷumâvi (Ep. Ind. Vol. VIII., p. 61).

At Nâsik, there are two inscriptions of Gautamîputra dated in the years 18 (insc. No. 1125 of Lüders's list) and 24 (insc. No. 1126). Professor D. R. Bhandarkar who has discussed this subject recently (Ind. Ant., Vol. XLVII, page 152) says : "Sir Ramkrishna Bhandarkar contends that all " these dates pertain to the reign of Puḷumâvi and that he " reigned conjointly with his father, the former over Mahâ- " râshṭra and the latter over the hereditary Śatavâhana " dominions. The latter view alone can be correct. For in in- " scription No. 5, Gautamiputra Śâtakarṇi, who is the donor " there along with his mother, issues a grant in favour of " Buddhist monks, who, it is expressly stated were staying in " the cave which was the pious gift of theirs. This cave which " was a pious gift of Śâtakarṇi and his mother must doubtless " be cave No. 3 which, as we have seen above, was excavated " and given over to the Bhadrâyaniyas. But then we have " also seen that this cave was presented to these monks in the " 19th regnal year, not of Śâtakarṇi but of Pulumâvi." " (Dekkan of the Śâtavâhana Period by Prof. D. R. Bhandar- " kar).

I regret I cannot accept this theory. On the contrary, the inscriptions themselves clearly show that Gautamîputra and Puḷumâvi have reigned in succession. Indeed, Gautamîputra, in the year 24, states distinctly that the cave was excavated under the orders of his mother and himself : "Pious gift of *ours*"; and in the inscription of queen Balaśrî in the 19th year of Puḷumâvi, the queen mother makes a solemn gift of the cave *in her own name*. This can be explained in only one way : the excavation of the cave was begun under the orders of Gautamî-putra and his mother before the 18th year of Gautamîputra and was finished only after the death of Gautamiputra and during the reign of his son Puḷumâvi; we have proof of it in the fact that it was the latter king that had it embellished with paintings. The cave not having been consecrated officially, this consecration took place only in the 19th year of Puḷumâvi. Since the king Gautamîputra was dead, the queen Balaśrî made the gift officially herself.

I have besides another remark to make on this occasion.

I think that the meaning of the inscription of the queen Balaśrî has not been correctly understood till now. We wonder why this inscription dated in the reign of Puḷumâvi contains exclusively the eulogies of Gautamiputra. I believe that the real meaning of the inscription, is this : the queen mother, when she was officially presenting the cave, cannot forget that it was under the orders of her son that the excavation of the cave was begun; it was therefore quite natural to eulogise the glorious Gautamîputra. Thus the inscription of Balaśrî has a clear meaning : it is the funeral oration on the great king delivered by an inconsolable mother.

Again the supposition that Gautamiputra was not the king of the region about Nâsik is untenable : 1) because Gautamîputra gives orders to the officers of Nâsik; 2) according to the inscription of Balaśrî he reigned over Surâshṭra, Aparânta, and, Vidarba; and Mr. Bhandarkar admits that he reigned also over the South; why should the Nâsik region alone form an exception? 3) We have seldom seen a father dating his grants in the reign (and especially in the 24th year) of the reign of his son ; 4) and lastly we have a positive proof of it in the hoard of Joghaltembhi.

We have said that this treasure consisted of 13250 coins bearing the name of Nahapâna of which 9270 had been restruck by Gautamîputra (J. B. B. R. A. S., Vol XXII, page 224). It is remarkable that in this treasure there is not a single coin of Vâsisṭhiputra Puḷumâvi who, as we know, has struck coins in his own name (see : Rapson, Coins of the Ândhra dynasty, page 20). As Joghaltembhi is a village in the environs of Nâsik, we have to conclude that, after the destruction of the Śakas, it was Gautamîputra that reigned in this place and that the treasure was buried during his reign and before the accession of Puḷumâvi. But Rev. H. R. Scott who has examined the hoard of Joghaltembhi carefully has made an important remark : "Judging from the condition of the coins, I should say that they must have been a very long time in circulation and that both before and *after* being counter-struck (J B. B. R. A. S., Vol XXII, p. 224); and he adds "They could not have been buried earlier than 20 years after Śâtakarṇi's victory". So, there is no doubt that Gautamîputra reigned in the Nâsik region for a long time, since the coins have had time to get considerably worn out. Puḷumâvi has therefore reigned at Nâsik for more than 15 years after the destruction of the Kshaharâtas.

It is certain that Chashṭana was for a time the contemporary of Puḷumâvi. In fact, Ptolemy says in his geography (Ind. Ant., Vol XIII., page 366) that Siro Polemaios reigned at Baithana, and Tiastanes at Ozênê. Ozênê is unquestionably Ujjain which was the capital of all the kings of the dynasty of Châshṭana, and Baithana is Paîṭana or Paîṭhana, the capital of Puḷumâvi. Unfortunately the evidence of Ptolemy dœs not enable us to know exactly in what epoch Chashṭana and Puḷumâvi lived. We do not know for certain in what year Ptolemy wrote his geography and we know little about the life of this scholar. Olympiodorus says that when Ptolemy was at Canopa in 147, he had already been making astronomical observations for 40 years, which will place Ptolemy's works between 104 and 147 A. D. Ptolemy was not a navigator; he was an astronomer of Alexandria who wrote his geography chiefly with the object of drawing a map of the world with latitudes and longitudes: and has he not the pretension to give his own views about the countries he speaks about. He confines himself to reconstructing the configuration of the countries, relying upon the descriptions given by the travellers in the works which can be had in his days. He himself admits that he follows Marin of Tyr, navigator who made his voyage about 100 A. D. From which book has Ptolemy taken his information about Puḷumâvi and Chasṭana? It may not be impossible that it was from the work of Marin of Tyr which unfortunately has not come down to us. But it is certain that this information was obtained from relatively recent sources and as Ptolemy wrote his geography in the first half of the IInd century, we may admit that the information he gives about Chashṭana and Puḷumâvi belongs to the beginning of the IInd century.

When the Kshaharâtas occupied Northern Deccan, the capital of the Śâtavâhanas was probably Amarâvatî on the lower course of the Kṛishṇâ. The legend that Śrî Kakulam was the capital has no foundation (see Ind. Ant., Nov. 1913, Vol XLII, page 276). At the time of Gautamîputra and at the beginning of the reign of Puḷumâvi it was Amarâvatî that was the capital : the king was called "Lord of Dhanamkaṭa" (insc. No. 3 at Nâsik. Dhanamkaṭa=Dhânyakaṭaka=Dhanakaṭa—Dhaññakaḍa). Puḷumâvi removed the capital to Paithana (Pratishṭhâna).

The Purâṇas pretend to give us the history of the Śâtavâhanas to whom they give the name of Ândhras. However, if we compare the information given in the Purâṇas with what is contained in the historical documents we possess, we find that it is only the Matsya that deserves to engage the attention of the historian. We shall not however attach any value to the durations of the reigns given in the Matsya Purâṇa, for, each time we proceed to verify these dates, "the Purâṇas are proved to be in error" (Vincent A. Smith.—Early History of India, 2d Edition, page 194). However the order of succession of the kings is nearer the truth. That order is as follows :

Gautamîputra,
Puḷomâ,
Śivaśrî,
Śivaskanda,
Yajñaśrî,
Vijaya,
Chaṇḍaśri Śântikarṇa,
Puḷomâ.

It is to be remarked that we find here Gautamîputra followed by Puḷumâvi; besides, the inscriptions and the coins are found to confirm the existence of Śivaśrî, of Yajñaśrî and of Chaṇḍa.

It is almost certain that the Matsya Purâṇa is right in saying that Śiva Śrî was the successor of Puḷumâvi, for we have (Rapson, page 29) the coins bearing the name "Raño Vâsiṭhiputa Siva-Siri-Sâtakaṁṇi (Vâsishṭhîputra Śiva-Śrî-Sâtakarṇi); and these coins are almost identical with those of Puḷumâvi in regard to the letters of the alphabet, the symbols (chaitya with three arches etc.) and the workmanship. We have also an inscription (No. 1279 of Lüder's list) of Amarâvatî which is dated in the reign of Siri-Sivamaka-Sada who is perhaps Śiva-Śri-Sâtakarṇi.

We have not yet found any documents, coins or inscriptions, mentioning Śivaskanda Sâtakaṇi. However, in cave 36 at Kaṇhêri, there is an inscription (No. 1001 of Lüders's list) dated in the 8th year of king Mâḍhariputa Svâmi whose name is followed by another not very legible which Mr. D. R. Bhandarkar (Ind. Ant. Vol XLVII, Part DXCVI, June 1918) has read Sri Sâta. The alphabet of this inscription (as well as of another, No. 1002) seems to show that this king reigned before Yajña Śrî. If this palæographical indication and the list given in the Matsya are correct, this Mâḍharîputra can be no other than Śivaskanda.

Yajña-Śri seems to have had a brilliant reign. It was in fact at the time of Gautamîputra Yajña Śâtakarṇi that was dug the chaitya of Kaṇhêri which is in a degenerate style compared with that of the splendid Chaitya at Kârli, but which is a remarkable monument (insc. No. 1124 of Lüders's list; 16th year of Yajña). It was also during the time of this king that was embellished the VIII cave at Nâsik whose inscription No. 4 is dated in the 7th year of his reign (Ep. Ind. Vol VIII., page 94). A fragment of a pillar discovered at China near the mouth of the Kṛishṇâ which has since been transported to the Madras Museum contains an inscription dated in the 27th year of the reign of Yajña (Ep. Ind., Vol. I., page 95): and the coins bearing the very characteristic name "Yajña" are also well known (see Rapson).

We know the name of Vijaya only from the Matsya Purâṇa.

Chaṇḍaśri Śantikarṇa must probably be identified with Vàsiṭhiputa Chadasâta who reigned at the time when the Koḍavolu inscription was engraved (see Report on Epigraphy; Madras Government orders; inscription No. 228 of 1908), and with Vâsisṭhiputa Siri Caḍa Sâti (Vâsishṭhîputra Śrî Chandra Śâti) of the coins (see Rapson, pages 30 and 32; Mr. Rapson thinks that this king must have preceded Yajña).

We shall speak of Puḷumâvi, the last king of this dynasty, in the following chapter concerning the Pallavas and the inscription at Myâkadoni.

The inscription (No. 965 of Lüders's list) of Girnar (Junâgaḍh in Kâṭhiâvâḍ) which is dated in the year 150 A. D. says [Ep. Ind. Vol VIII., p. 47] that Rudradâman, by his own valour [svavîryy-ârjjitânâm] gained Âkarâvantî (Mâḷwâ), Surâshṭra (Kâṭhiâwâṛ), Kachchha (Cutch), Aparânta (the coast to the north of Bombay) etc, destroyed the Yaudhêyas, who were loath to submit, defeated Śâtakarṇi, lord of Dakshinâpatha, but on account of the nearness of their connection did not destroy him but himself acquired the name of Mahâkshatrapa.

Which king of the Śâtavâhana dynasty is called here by the name of Śâtakarṇi ? The inscriptions and the coins seem to confirm the statement of the Girnar inscription. An inscription at Kaṇhêri (No. 994 of Lüders's list) "exhibits the neat characters of Western Kshatrapa inscriptions" (Bühler, Ind. Ant., Vol XXXIII, page 43). This inscription, as those of Rudradâman is in Sanskṛit and thus differs from all other Śâtavâhana inscriptions which are all in Prâkṛit. This inscription mentions the queen of Vâsishṭhîputra Sri Sâtakarṇi, daughter of the mahâkshatrapa Ru[dra]. The last name consists only of two syllables the first of which is certainly "Ru" and the second very probably "dra." Secondly Yajña Śri "issued coins......and they are similar in fabric and style to the Kshatrapa coins" (Rapson, section 87). The characteristic of these coins is that the head of king Yajña is represented on them, whereas the image of the king is not found in any coin of the other Śâtavâhanas. It is therefore certain that it is Yajña who adopted the Kshatrapa style for these coins. These coins of Yajña (Rapson Pl.VII., El) resemble those of Rudradâman. It has to be remarked that the coif of Rudradâman found on his coins resembles that of Yajña; it is a sort of spherical calotte covering the skull and differs totally from the coif of Chashṭana; and the sculptures of the chaitya of Kaṇhêri which are dated in the time of Yajña show us personages who have their hair dressed as Yajña and Rudradâman. It is therefore probable that it was Rudradâman who adopted the coiffure that was used in the Deccan at the time of Yajña Sri. Thus then Rudradâman was almost a contemporary of Yajña and was besides the father-in-law of a Vâsishṭhiputra Śâtakarṇi, which Yajña was not, as we know that he was a Gautamiputra. Unfortunately we know three Śâtavâhanas who bore the name of Vasishṭhiputra : the great Puḷumâvi, Śiva Sri and Chanda Śri. We know also a certain Vasishthîputra Chatarapana who had reigned 13 years when an inscription at Nânâghâṭ (No. 1120 of Lüders's list) was engraved; it is however probable that this latter

Vâsishṭhiputra is no other than Śiva-Śrî or Chanda Śrî, and the word Chaturapana is suspicious (see J. R. A. S. for 1905, page 798).

It is almost certain that the Vâsishthiputra who was the son-in-law of Rudradâman was not the great Puḷumâvi: we know in fact that Puḷumâvi was the contemporary of Chashṭana. It appears therefore to be impossible that he should have married the great-grand-daughter of Chashṭana. There yet remain Śiva Śrî and Chanda Śrî; but it is probable that the son-in-law of Rudradâman was rather Śiva Śrî, who might have married the daughter of Rudradâman after having fought with him once and who might have been defeated in his turn about the year 130 A. D., when fighting a second time with the Kshatrapa king. Rudradâman might have been the victor and might have occupied Aparânta for some time up to the reign of Yajña Srî who might have adopted into this region a coinage similar to that of Rudradâman. The above are suppositions, since the documents we have do not enable us to have a correct knowledge of this history.

The following might perhaps be the chronology of the Sâtavâhanas in conjunction with that of the Western Kshatrapas:

Circ. A. D.	
78	Destruction of Kshaharâtas by Gautamiputra.
79	1st year of the reign of Chashṭana and of the Saka era; Circ. 10th year of the reign of Gautamîputra.
From 95 to 120	Reigns of Puḷumâvi and Chashṭana.
From 120 to 140	Invasion of the Yaudhêyas and of the Ândhras; Jayadâman transfers his power to his son Rudradâman who gets the title of Mahâkshatrapa and defeats Śiva Srî Sâtakarṇi.
From 140 to 150	Rudradâman occupies Aparânta; reign of Śivaskanda.
From 150 to 155	End of the reign of Rudradâman; beginning of the reign of Yajña Srî.
From 155 to 178	Reign of Dâmajadaśrî and of Yajña Śrî
From 178 to 180	End of the reign of Yajña Śrî and beginning of the reigns of Jîvadâman and Vijaya Śâtakarṇi.

In the above chronology we have admitted that Rudradâman was the contemporary of a series of three kings:

(1) Vâsishthiputra Śiva Śrî,
(2) Mâḍharîputra Sivaskanda,
(3) Gautamiputra Yajña Śrî.

But some coins found in the Kolhapur region (Rapson, pages 5, 7, 14) have restrucks which enables us to settle the following series :

(1) Vâsishthiputra Vilivâyakura,
(2) Mâḍhariputra Sivalakura,
(3) Gautamiputra Vilivâyakura,

Can these two series be identified ?

It is to be remarked that :

(1) The first names, Vâsishthiputra, Mâḍharîputra, Gautamîputra, prove nothing, as we know that these names indicate a Gôtra and the custom of prefixing to the real name of a person the name of his mother's Gôtra has been in existence in the dynasties of the neighbours of the Śâtavâhanas (the Âbhiras, the Chuṭus, the Ikshvâkus). There then remain the second names, and they, Vilivâyakura and Sivalakura, have not been found in authentic Śâtavâhana inscriptions.

(2) The coins bear as symbols "bow and arrow" in place of the Ujjain symbol of the coins of Śâtavâhanas.

(3) Again, these coins have been found only in the Kolhapur region; and Ptolemy says, that at Hippokura, in a country which may be situated approximately in this part of the Deccan, there reigned a king named Baleokuros, who, many authors have believed, can be identified with Vilivâyakura. This king will, in that case, be a contemporary of Puḷumâvi and belong to another dynasty.

I think therefore that these coins may be provisionally admitted to belong to the "Kolhapur Dynasty."

Some coins bearing the names of Srî Rudra Sâtakarṇi and Sri Kṛishṇa Śâtakarṇi have been found (see Rapson, Coins of Indian Museum; Ândhra dynasty) in the Chanda district of the Central Provinces. As these names have been found only in this region, we may suppose that these kings belonged to a peculiar dynasty that subsisted for some time in the Chanda district, when the Śâtavâhanas had been replaced by the Chuṭus, the Nâgas, the Pallavas, the Ikshvâkus and the Bṛihatphalâyanas.

CHAPTER III

THE PALLAVAS.

§ I. The Pallava mystery.

In "The Oxford History of India" which Mr. Vincent A. Smith has published this year (Oxford, 1919), he says (page 205); "The Pallavas constitute one of the mysteries of Indian history" and again in his "Early History of India" (2nd edition, page 423) he has said: "Who were the Pallavas ? Whence did they come ? How did they attain the chief place among the powers of the South ? "

Many authors have answered this question with a theory [see the Mysore Gaz., I., pages 303-4; see also Madras Manual, I., page 129] which may be called "The theory of Parthian invasion". The supporters of this theory believe that the Pallavas were a northern tribe of Parthian origin, that they were a clan of nomads who, having come from Persia, were not able to settle in Northern India and so continued their invasion up to Kâñchipuram. This hypothesis was very charming to the imagination. They pictured to themselves a number of men of the white race, the Parthians, brandishing their bows (the Parthian arrow is well-known) forming a nomadic tribe, transporting their camp from country to country and destroying, like the Huns, everthing they found on their way. It is thus they would have traversed the whole of India and would have stopped only at the extremity of the Peninsula. Then, after having vanquished the ancient tribes in the South, they would have established their capital at Kâñchipuram. This theory presents a very great dificulty. This great invasion, by a whole clan of the Parthian tribe, extending from the frontiers of Persia to the extreme South of the Indian peninsula, implies an immense political commotion in the Deccan. When did this important event take place ? Certain authors, and V. Venkayya in particular, have tried to determine "the date of the Pallava migration to the South". But up to the present day we have not found any document which proves the existence of a Parthian invasion of Southen India. We may say that this theory makes the Pallava mystery still more mysterious. It is not therefore without cause that Mr. Vicent A. Smith, in the two last editions of his "Early History of India", has abandoned the theory of the Parthian invasion and has tried to discover a less improbable theory.

"There is every reason to believe that future historians will be able to give a fairly complete narrative of the doings of the Pallava kings, and that the mystery which surrounds their origin and affinities may be elucidated in large measure." (The Oxford History of India, page 210).

It is with the object of realising the wish of Mr. Vincent A. Smith that we now proceed to prove the following propositions :

(1) The Ândhra empire was governed by feudatories who bore the title of Mahârathis and were called "Nâgas" as they belonged to a race of serpent-worshippers.

(2) Coins containing the image of a "Ship with two masts" are found almost exclusively on the coast between Madras and Cuddalore and they represent the moneys of Toṇḍai-Maṇḍalam of which Kañchi is the capital. According to Prof. Rapson, these coins bear the legend "Śri Puḷumâvi". The Ujjain symbol indicates the Śâtavâhana dynasty. So this dynasty reigned over the territory of Kâñchipuram. Further, an inscription of Puḷumâvi, the last king of that dynasty, shows that the prince Skanda-Nâga was his great general ; there is no doubt that the Nâgas were very powerful when the Śâtavahâna dynasty came to an end.

(3) It is certain that one of those royal families of Nâga origin, the "Chuṭu", took the place of the Śâtavâhanas.

(4) It is certain that all the most ancient Pallava kings

were the contemporaries of the Chuṭus of the Nâga race.

(5) It is also certain that the Pallavas succeeded the Chuṭus of the Nâga race.

(6) The Pallava plates of Vêlûrpâḷaiyam contain (verses 3 to 22) the history of the Pallavas according to the family tradition. There, it is said that the first member of the family who become king "acquired all the emblems of royalty on marrying the daughter of the lord of Serpents——evidently a Nâga princess" (Report on Epigraphy for 1910—1911; G. O. Public, 28th July, Part II, No. 7, page 61).

(7) I hold the theory that I have enunciated in my work "The Pallavas" (Pondicherry, 1917): "The earliest Pallavas were not kings, and they were alien to South India. One of them married the daughter of one of the kings of that country and thus became a king himself" (The Pallavas, page 23). At the time of the Girnar inscription the Western Satrapas reigned in Âparânta and had a Pahlava for their minister. These Pahḷavas were the neighbours of the Nâgas when the Chuṭu-Nâgas reigned in Aparânta (Kaṇhêri inscription of the mother of Skanda-Nâga, No. 1021 of Lüders's list). A Pallava prince married the daughter of the King Śiva-Skanda-Nâga-Śâtakarṇi, and inherited the throne of Kâñchî.

Such, in a few words, is our theory in regard to the origin of the Pallavas. We shall now proceed to develop it.

No. 1. Mahârathis, Chuṭus, Nâgas.

The inscription of Nânâghât (Arch. Surv. West. Ind. Vol. V, No. 3, p. 64) says that Śâtakarṇi, king of Dakshinâpatha married Nâga-Nikâ, daughter of a Mahârathi Kaḷalâya.

The "lion pillar" at Kârlî (Ep. Ind. Vol., VII., page 49) was a gift of Mahârathi Agni-Mitra-Nâga.

After the fall of the Śâtavâhana dynasty, a large portion of the empire passed into the hands of the dynasty of the Chuṭus who were related to the Mahârathis. The Chuṭus and the Mahârathis often bore the title of Śâtakarṇis.

An inscription (No. 1195 of Lüders's list) at Maḷavalli in the Shikârpur taluq of Mysore (Ep. Carn., Vol. VII., Sk.

263; plate facing the page 252. See also "Mysore and Coorg from inscriptions", plate facing page 21) is dated in the 2nd year of the reign of Hâritiputa-Vinhukaḍa-Chuṭukulananda Sâtakaṁṇi, king of Vaijayanti. We know that Vaijayanti is nothing but Banavâsi and this very town of Banavâsi contains an inscription (No. 1186 of Lüders's list; see also Arch. Surv. West. Ind., Vol IV., Pl. IV.; and Ind. Ant., 1885, 331) which is dated in the 12th year of the same king: "According to Dr. Burgess, account........., it is carved "on the two edges of a large slate slab, bearing the represent- "ation of a five-hooded cobra." (Ind. Ant., Vol. XIV, p. 331). According to Bühler (Ind. Ant, Vol. XIV, p. 332) "the alphabet "resembles, as Dr. Bhagwanlal Indraji has stated, that of the "Nâsik inscription of Siriyaña-Sâtakaṁṅi". This king bears here the same name as in the Maḷavalli inscription. However, there is this important thing to be remarked here, that the name of the family is given here as Viṇhukaḍaḍuṭu instead of Viṇhukaḍachuṭu, the word Dutu is therefore synonymous with Chuṭu. We know (see Rapson, page 59 and Pl. VIII., No. 235) some coins of a king called Dhuṭukaḷânanda who belonged surely to the dynasty of the Chuṭus.

The inscription of Banavâsi says that king Śâṭakarṇi had a daughter who joined her son in making gift of a Nâga. The son was called Śâta or Śivaskanda-Nâga-Srî. An inscription at Kaṇhêri (No. 1021 of Lüders's list), is a donation by Nâga-Mula-Nikâ who was the daughter of the "great king" that reigned at this epoch. She was the wife of a Mahâraṭhi and a more important detail is that she was the mother of prince Skanda-Nâga-Sâta. Mr. Rapson writing on this subject says (page LIII): "there can be no doubt that she is to be identified with the donor mentioned in the following inscription from Banavasi and that she was, therefore, the daughter of king Haritiputra Vishṇukada Cuṭu Śatakarṇi whose name must have stood originally in the present inscription". Kaṇhêri being situated in Aparânta, there can be no doubt that the Chuṭus succeeded the Ândhras not only in Mysore but also in Aparânta, near Bombay.

The prince Skanda-Nâga-Śâtaka or Śivaskanda-Nâga was not a Chuṭu because his mother was a Chuṭu princess. His father was a Mahâraṭhi; to which dynasty did he belong? It is probable that he was a descendant of the kings that reigned over the territory of Chitaldroog. We know that Chitaldroog is only about fifty miles east of Banavâsi, where we find the inscription of Śivaskanda-Nâga-Sâta, and to the west of Chitaldroog, on the site of an ancient city whose name is said to have been Chandrâvali where found in 1888 some leaden coins (Ep. Ind. Vol VII, p. 51, see plate III, fig A, B, C; and Rapson; Pl. VIII, No. 233 et page 57) which bear the name of Sadakana-Kaḷalâya-Mahâraṭhi. The emblems are, on the obverse, a humped bull standing, and on the reverse, tree and chaitya. This Sadakaṇa (Śatâkarṇṇi) who bears the title of Mahâraṭhi is probably an ancestor of Mahâraṭhi Satakana or Śâta who made the grant of a Nâga at Banavâsi. In fact, both of them are Mahâraṭhis; they have the same title of Sâta, and they have both reigned in the same country, in the vicinity of Maḷavalli and Chitaldroog. The kings of this country were Nâgas; Mr. Rice says (Mysore and Coorg from inscriptions " page 202): "The early inhabitants of the country were " probably to a great extent, specially on the female side, Nâgas, " or serpent worshippers, that is, of the cobra, which is the " Nâga......In the Śâtavâhana inscription of Banavâsi of the " first or second century, the king's daughter is named Nâgaśri " and she makes the gift of a Nâga". We may add that this queen is named Nâga-Mula-Nikâ in the Kaṇhéri inscription, that her son's name was Skanda-Nâga-Sata; that the Banavâsi inscription is engraved beside the image of a Nâga; and that the country around Maḷavalli and Banavâsi was once called Nâgakhanda. It is probable that these Mahâraṭhis-Nâgas who bore, like the Ândhras, the title of Śâtakarṇi, are the Ândhrabhṛityas or servants of the Ândhras, who, as mentioned in the Purâṇas, succeeded the Śâtavahanas.

The Myâkadoni inscription (Report on Epigraphy for 1915—16; Madras, G. O. No. 99; 29th Aug 1916, Part II, No. 1, page 112—inscription No. 509 of Apendix B.——See also Ep. Ind. Vol. XIV., page 153) says that this village was in the territory governed by the great general (Mahâsênâpati) Kaṁdanâka (Skanda-Nâga) and we know that Myâkadoni is not far from Chitaldroog. The Myàkadoni inscription is dated in the 8th year of the reign of Siri-Puḷumâvi. Who is this Pulumâvi? It is noteworthy that we do not find here the name Vâsisṭhîputra which is peculiar to the inscriptions of the son of Gautamiputra. Besides, the alphabet of the Myâkadoni inscription is much less archaic than that of the inscriptions of great Puḷumâvi. Mr. V. S. Sukthankar of Poona who has edited the Myâkadoni inscription has observed this detail: "The alphabet resembles that of the Joggayyapeṭa inc. of Purisadata" (Ep. Ind. Vol. XIV., page 153); and the inscriptions of Purisadata at Jaggayyapeṭa have been attributed to the III century by all the authors who have spoken of it and no one doubts that Purisadata reigned after the Śâtavâhanas. The alphabet of the Myâkadoni inscription is incontestably much more developed than the alphabets of all the other Śâtavâhana inscriptions and very much resembles those of the Chuṭus and the ancient Pallavas. It is therefore very probable that the Puḷumâvi of the Myâkadoni inscription is the last king of the Śâtavahana dynasty in the list given in the Matsya Purâṇa. The only objection that can be raised, is that the inscription is dated in the 8th year of his reign, whereas the Matsya Purâṇa gives him only a reign of 7 years. But we have already said that we must not rely on the duration of the reigns given in the Matsya Purâna; this objection is therefore worthless, and there are reasons to think that the Myâkadoni inscription is dated in the reign of the last of the Śatavâhanas. In any case, we may affirm that this Puḷumâvi is not the son of Gautamiputra. We know the alphabet of this king from the Nâsik and Amarâvati inscriptions; and there is a very great difference between them and that of Myâkadoni; I believe that there must be an interval of more than a century between the two Puḷumâvis, and that the Puḷumâvi of Myâkadoni is certainly one of the later Śâtavâhanas. The discovery of the Myâkadoni inscription has a very important bearing on this subject; it enlightens the causes of the fall of the Śâtavâhana dynasty: we learn, in fact, that in the 8th year of the last king of this dynasty, a certain Skanda-Nâga was the Mahâsênâpati — that is to say the military governor — of all the country extending to the South of the Tuṅgabhadra not far from Chiṭaldroog and Banavâsi.

Śiva-Skanda-Nâga who is mentioned in the Banavâsi inscription had probably a glorious reign, as, even in the time of the Kadambas, they remembered his name: in fact, an inscription at Maḷavalli (No. 1196 of Lüders's list), which is surely an inscription of an ancient Kadamba king, says that king Śivaskandavarman reigned over that country at one time (see the Plate in Ep. Carn. Vol. VII., facing the page 252).

Further, the celebrated Kadamba inscription at Tâḷguṇḍa mentions a Śiva temple in that town "at which Śâtakarṇi and other kings had formerly worshipped" (Ep. Ind., Vol VIII., page 24).

We do not know any other name given to this dynasty except that of Śâtakarnṇi-Śiva-Skanda-Nâga.

The same Tâḷguṇḍa inscription says that Mayûraśarman, the first king of the Kadamba dynasty, conquered the country by fighting with the Pallavas. It is therefore certain that the Nâgas were succeeded by the Pallavas.

No. 2—The early Pallava kings.

Three sets of copper-plates written in Prâkṛit in a very archaic alphabet prove that, in the III century of the Christian era, there reigned on the southern banks of the Kṛishṇâ, the dynasty of the Pallavas of Bhâradvâja gôtra who had Kâñchîpuram for their capital.

(1) The plates found at Mayidavôlu (Guntûr district) (Ep. Ind. Vol. VI., page 84) say that in the 10th year of the reign of his father whose name is not given, the heir-apparent (Yuva-mahârâja) Śivaskandavarman gave an order to the governors of Dhaññakada, i. e. Amarâvati.

(2) The plates (Ep. Ind., Vol I., page 2) found at Hirahaḍagalli (Bellary district) are dated in the 8th year of the reign of Śivaskandavarman who confirms a gift made by his father whose name is not given, but who is designated by the title of Bappa-dêva. These plates mention the province of Sâtâhani which we know (from the Myâkadoni inscription) to be a portion of the Bellary district.

(3) The plates found in the Guntûr district (Ep. Ind. Vol. VIII., page 143) are dated in the reign of Vijayaskandavarman and commemorate a grant made by Chârudêvi, wife of the heir-apparent (Yuva-mahârâja) Vijaya-Buddhavarman and mother of a prince whose name ends in "kura". J. F. Fleet

who was the first to edit these plates in the Indian Antiquary (see plate facing page 101 and note 23, page 101) has said: "two letters, containing the first part of a proper name, are illegible here". Dr. Hultzsch, in reediting this document, believed he could read the whole name as Buddhyaṅkura. In that case, it seems to be a surname and not the name.

It is possible to identify Yuva-Mahâràja Śiva-Skandavarman of Mâyidâvolu with the king Śiva-Skandavarman of Hirahaḍagalli. The king is called Śiva-Skandavarman in the Hirahaḍagalli plates and Vijaya-Skandavarman in those of the Guntûr district. But the words Śiva and Vijaya are prefixes and we shall see in the Kadamba documents such names as Śiva-Mṛigèśavarman Śiva-Mândhâtṛivarman, and also Śiva-Kṛishṇa (Bennur plates; Belur, 245; Ep. Carn., Vol. V). We find even the prefix Śri-Vijaya-Śiva (Ep. Carn., Vol VII., page 7.). Besides, a similar identification has been made in regard to the dynasty of the Nâgas: we have identified Śiva-Skanda-Nâga of Banavâsi with Skanda-Nâga of Kaṇhêri. The alphabet of the Hirahaḍagalli plates closely resembles that of Charudêvi's grant.

I therefore think that there is no serious difficulty in putting together the three documents, Mâyidâvôlu, Hirahaḍagalli and Guntûr district and establishing the following genealogy:

A king
(designated by the title of "Bappa-Dêva" in the Hirahaḍagalli plates)

|

The king Skandavarman
(with the prefix Śiva in the Mâyidavôlu and Hirahaḍagalli plates; and with the prefix Vijaya in the plates of the Guntûr district.)

|

The prince Buddhavarman
(with the prefix "Vijaya"; husband of Charudêvi)

|

A prince
(designated by the surname of [Buddhyaṅ]kura in the plates of the Guntûr district).

In what epoch did these princes reign? It is certain that they succeeded the Sâtavâhanas: in fact, the three documents prove that they reigned on the southern bank of the Kṛishṇâ (particularly at Amarâvatî) and in the Sâtâhani district; since the Śâtavâhana dynasty probably subsisted up to the first quarter of the III century, and since the Mâyidavôlu plates are certainly contemporaneous with those of Kondamûdi [it is certain that these plates were engraved, as we shall see, shortly after the fall of the Ândhras] it is probable that the king surnamed Bappa-dêva reigned in the second quarter of the III century (225-250 A. D.).

On the other hand we know that in 338 A. D. Samudra-Gupta had as his adversary a king of Kâñchî named Vishṇu-gôpa. This king was therefore probably an immediate successor of [Buddhyaṅ]kura, if this prince ascended the throne.

Thus then, with the historical information in our possession, we can imagine the following chronology :

(1) "Bappa-dêva" . . . 2nd quarter of the III century.
(2) Skandavarman . . 3rd quarter of the III century.
(3) Buddhavarman . . 4th quarter of the III century.
(4) [Buddhyaṅ]kura. . 1st quarter of the IV century.
(5) Vishṇugôpa . . . 2nd quarter of the IV century.

No. 3—The origin of the Pallavas.

Before handling the subject of the origin of the Pallavas, we must here specify an important point.

If we suppose that the word "Pallava" signifies a tribe, we must inquire by which invasion this tribe got possession of the kingdom of Kâñchîpuram; if, we admit that the word "Pallava" is the name of a family, it is enough, to explain the presence of the Pallavas in Kâñchî, to find out by what political event one of the members of this family succeeded to the throne; here, no doubt is possible, because, the Mâyidavôlu, Hirahaḍagalli and Guntûr district plates, which come up to the III century of the Christian era, never mention a Pallava nation but only speak of a royal family one of whose members was king at Kâñchî, and we shall now proceed to answer the following question : what political event was it that placed on the throne a prince who belonged to a family named "Pallava"?

In 1917 ("The Pallavas", page 23,) I drew the attention of the readers to a document which I think can give us the key to this problem : verse 6 of the Vêlûrpâḷaiyam plates, (S. I. I., Vol II, Part V; page 510) in giving a summary of the history of the Pallavas, says that the first member of this dynasty that became king, got the throne by marrying the daughter of a Nâga king and that the son born of this union was named Skanda. Can this tradition that we find in the Pallava documents be verified by authentic history?

A large number of coins having for emblems the "ship with two masts" on the obverse and the "Ujjain symbol" on the reverse has been found on the Coromandel coast between Madras and Cuddalore. These ship-coins seem to be special to that part of the coast that is in the neighbourhood of Kâñchîpuram. The "Ujjain symbol" indicates the Śâtavâhana dynasty. Mr. Rapson (page 22) has been able to decipher the inscription on these coins ; he has read it to be "Śrî Puḷumâvi"; thus, all that part of the Coromandel coast which is in the vicinity of Kâñchipuram was under the domination of the Śâtavâhanas. So, the Pallavas established themselves at Kâñchipuram after the Śâtavâhanas. The alphabet of the Mâyidavôlu plates proves that Śiva-Skandavarman was nearly contemporary of the last Ândhra kings. So, it is at the time of the fall of the Śâtavâhanas that a member of the Pallava family ascended the throne of Kâñchi; it is quite possible that this first king was "Bappa-dêva" father of Śiva-Skandavarman. We also note that the son of "Bappa-dêva" was called Skanda and tradition has it that the first Pallava king having married a Nâga princess had a son named Skanda.

When speaking of the famous inscription of Bala-Śrî at Nâsik, we have said that Gautamîputra vanquished the Palhavas (Ep. Ind., Vol VIII., Pl I, No. 2, line 5) in 78 A. D. Again, we learn from the Girnar inscription that Suviśâkha who was the minister of Rudradâman in 150 A. D. was a Pahlava (Junagadh inscription; Ep. Ind., Vol VIII., page 37 and Plate line 19). Thus the word which was written Palhava in 78 A. D. was written Pahlava in 150 A. D., and we note, when whe see the Girnar inscription, that the compound letter "hla" resembles the double ll. Besides, in Mâyidavôlu plates written in Prâkṛit: this question of letters has been solved in a very simple manner they wrote Palava. This can correspond to Pallava for in Prâkṛit the consonants are not doubled. In the Hirahaḍagalli plates it is written as Pallava though they are also in Prâkrit. Later on, when the documents were written in Sanskṛit, the word Pallava will be understood to mean "sprout". The identity of names leads us to think that the ancient kings of Kâñchî belonged to the same family as the minister of Rudradâman. He lived in 150 A. D. and we know Pallava kings reigning at Kâñchî in aboui 225 A. D. How did a member of this family that we find in Surâshṭra in 150 A. D. establish himself in Kâñchî ? The Vêlûrpâḷaiyam plates give the answer to this question : a Pallava became king by marrying the daughter of a Nâga king : and all the documents in our possession regarding the Nâgas and the Pallavas seem to confirm this proposition. The Girnar inscription says that Rudradâman reigned in the province of Aparânta, that is, in the neighbourhood of Kaṇhêri, and that his minister was a Pahlava : and it is in this same Aparânta in Kaṇhêri that we find : (1) the inscription of the daughter of Rudradâman, (2) the inscription of Nâga-Mula-Nika, mother of Skanda-Nâga-Śâtakarṇi. The latter inscription is written in such an archaic alphabet that it was first believed to be an inscription of Puḷumâvi (Rapson, page LIII). Thus the minister of Rudradâman and the mother of the Nâga prince have lived almost at the same time and in the same country. We must not forget that the daughter of Rudradâman married a Śâtakarṇi. Moreover, the Hîrahaḍagalli plates have been found in the Bellary district, not far from Chitaldroog, where have been found the coins of the Mahârathis; these plates are written in an alphabet almost identical with that of the Banavâsi inscription; the Hirahaḍagalli plates are dated in the reign of Śiva-Skanda-Pallava and the Banavâsi inscription mentions Śiva-Skanda-Nâga. Thus the Nâgas were the neighbours and the contemporaries of the Pallavas.

There is again a very peculiar point of resemblance between these two dynasties; we have said that Śiva-Skanda-Nâga was a Mahâraṭhi who reigned in the Chitaldroog region where the coins of a Mahâraṭhi have been found. These coins bear for emblem a "humped bull standing" (Ep. Ind. Vol. VII, page 51, plate III., figures A, B, C; and Rapson, Pl. VIII, No. 233, and page 57), and it is the "humped well standing" that is represented in the seals of the Guntûr district plates of Skandavarman (see Ep. Ind., Vol VIII, plate facing page 144); we know that the bull was the crest of the Pallavas.

All that we have said above seem to show that a Pallava prince who was a native of the territory adjoining Aparânta married the daughter of Śiva-Skanda-Nâga, and became king of Kâñchi, after the downfall of the Śâtavâhana dynasty; and that the son born of the marriage of the first Pallava king with the Nâga princess bore, according to the custom of the Hindus, the name of his grandfather Śiva-Skanda.

Upon the whole, the history of the Deccan in the III century is not well understood; however, all the documents in our possession seem to show that in the first quarter of the III century the last Śâtavâhana king was called Pulumâvi; the empire was governed by the Maharaṭhis who belonged to certain families that were related to one another and bore the names of Chuṭu, Nâga and Pallava; it is these families that replaced the Śâtavâhanas.

§ 2. The expedition of Samudra-Gupta.

We know that a pillar in the fort of Allâhâbâd contains an inscription which is not dated but which has been engraved during the reign of Samudra-Gupta. This inscription which is intended to glorify the emperor and which gives us the history of his reign has been published by J. F. Fleet in his work "Gupta inscriptions".

The interpretation of this inscription has given room to numerous errors and some of them great ones. A few of them have been corrected. For instance, the text contains the word "Kaurâḷa"; Fleet (Gupta Insc., page 7, footnote 1.) has said that this word "is obviously a mistake" and has corrected it into "Kairaḷa" and then into Kêraḷa; thence it has been concluded that Samudra-Gupta advanced as far as the Chêra kingdom in South India. This identification of Kaurâḷa with the Malabar coast seemed to be confirmed by two other identifications : Kauṭṭura with Kôṭṭûra=Pollâchi (Coimbatôre District) [see J. R. A. S., 1897, page 29] and Palakka with Pâlghât. But now Kauṭṭura is identified with Kothoor in Ganjâm, and Palakka with a capital of the same name which was situated to the South of the Kṛishṇâ and which is mentioned in many Pallava copper-plates (J. R. A. S., 1905, page 29). Moreover, I have myself, in 1917, in my work "The Pallavas," pages 14 and 15, said that the Pallavas reigned on the banks of the Kṛishṇâ having their capital at Kâñchî; so, Samudra-Gupta was able to fight with Vishṇugôpa of Kâñchî without any necessity to advance to the capital : and I ventured the opinion that they probably met on the banks of the Kṛishṇâ and perhaps even in the north of the river as we may suppose that the Pallava king went forward to meet the Gupta emperor. Thus Samudra-Gupta's expedition turns out to be considerably reduced. However, I think that there are yet numerous errors to be corrected and that the whole history of Samudra-Gupta must be set right.

(1) Mr. Vincent A. Smith believes that Samudra-Gupta carried on his campaign in the valley of the Ganges before making that of the Deccan and that the latter ended about 350 A. D. However, the author of the inscription speaks of the expedition against the kings of Dakshiṇâpatha before speaking of the expedition against the kings of Âryyâvartta. I cannot but think that he has followed the chronological order; I am therefore of opinion that the expedition to the south took place at the beginning of the reign, about 335 or 340 A. D.

(2) Certain authors affirm that the hill Mahêndragiri is mentioned in the inscription. However, the passage "paishṭapurakamahendragirikauṭṭurakasvâmidatta" means: Mahêndra of Paishṭapura and Svâmidatta of Girikauṭṭura, that is to say, the fort of Koṭṭûra which is on the hill. There is therefore no reference in the inscription to the hill named Mahêndragiri.

(3) Mr. Kielhorn in studying the Aihole inscription (Ep. Ind., Vol. VI., No. 1, page 3) has identified "the water of Kunâḷa" mentioned in this inscription with the kingdom of Kaurâḷa mentioned in the Allâhâbâd inscription. This interpretation has been adopted without any discussion and now everybody admits that Samudra-Gupta defeated the king who was reigning "on the banks of the Kollêru (Colair) lake." I do not however see any reason why Kaurâḷa should be identified with Kunâḷa. The names themselves do not resemble each other. I think that the word Kaurâḷa must be read as Korâḷa and must be translated as "the Korâḷa kingdom" and that the Colair lake is not mentioned in the Allâhâbâd inscription.

(4) In 1898 (J. R. A. S., 1898, page 369) Fleet affirmed that Airaṇḍapalla must be identified with Eraṇḍôl, the chief town of a subdivision of the same name in the Khândêsh district of the Bombay Presidency. The only poof was the similarity of the names. At once, all the historians admitted this interpretation and supposed that Samudra-Gupta, after having gone as far as Kâñchi returned to the North of India travelling through the vicinity of Bombay; and then, they identified the "Daivarâstra" of the Allâhâbâd inscription with Mahârâshṭra.

This identification of Airaṇḍapalla with Eraṇḍôl is surely wrong. In the Allâhâbâd inscription, Airaṇḍapalla is mentioned immediately after the citadel of Koṭṭûra hill; it is therefore on the coast of Orissa that we must search for Eraṇḍapalla. The

Siddhantam plates of Dêvêndravarman (Ep. Ind. Vol. XII, page 212) were issued to make a grant to an inhabitant of Eraṇḍapali, a town probably near Chicacole and which is, in all likelihood, the Airandapalla of the inscription of Samudra-Gupta.

(5) The identification of Dêvarashtra with Mahàràshṭra is quite wrong. A set of copper-plates discovered in 1908-9 (No. 14) at Kâsimkôṭa in the district of Vizagapatam mentions the grant made by the E. Chalukya king Bhima I. of a village situated in Elamañcha Kalingadêśa which formed part of the province called Dêvaràshṭra. "Elamañchi-Kalingadêśa is perhaps to be " interpreted as "the Kalinga-country of which Elamañchi " (The modern Yellamanchili) was the chief town" (see Report on Epigraphy for 1908-1909; G.O. n. 538; 28 July 1909. Part II, No. 59, page 109).

To conclude: a)Airandappalla is situated in the Ganjam district and Dêvaràshṭra is in the Vizagapatam district. I think I have now proved that Samudra-Gupta never went to the western part of the Deccan.

So the Allâhâbâd inscription does not at all speak of Kêraḷa, Pollâchi, Pâlghât, Mahêndragiri, Colair lake, Eraṇḍôl in Kândêsh and Mahârâshṭra. All the kingdoms mentioned in the inscription are situated on the east coast of the Deccan. The expedition was solely confined to this coast. How far did Samudra-Gupta advance? Since Vishṇugôpa of Kâñchi reigned on the banks of the Kṛishnâ it is probable that he met with Samudra-Gupta in that region.

(6) It has always been admitted till now that the expedition of Samudra-Gupta was a very glorious one. However the inscription contains a detail which indicates the contrary; in fact, it is said that Samudra-Gupta captured the kings and afterwards released them; and it is confirmed by the fact that none of the kingdoms of the Deccan remained in the possession of the Guptas. It is probable that Samudra-Gupta first subjugated some kings, but that very soon he encountered superior forces and was therefore obliged to relinquish his conquests and return rapidly to his own state. After all those rectifications that we have just made, the expedition of Samudra-Gupta presents itself before our eyes in quite another form: it is no more a new Alexander marching victoriously through South

India ; it was simply the unfortunate attempt of a king from the North who wanted to annex the coast of Orissa but completely failed. About A. D. 340, Samudra-Gupta left his capital Pâṭaliputra and marched directly towards the South. First he conquered Southern Kôsala where the king Mahêndra was reigning in the vicinity of Sirpur and Sombalpur. He then crossed the forests that are to the south of Sonpur and found there the small kingdom of Mahâkântára which means "the great forest" and where Vyâghra-râja, "the tiger king" was reigning. Then he reached the coast of Orissa. Maṇṭarâja, king of Korâḷa, Mahêndra of Pishṭapura, Svâmidatta of Koṭṭúra, a citadel on the top of a hill, and Damana of Eraṇḍapali tried to stop him but were captured. Samudra-Gupta now prepared to make new conquests when he was opposed by a confederacy of all the kings that reigned near the mouths of the Gôdâvari and the Kṛishṇâ, the most powerful of them being Vishṇugôpa, the Pallava king of Kâñchi. The other kings were Nilarâja of Âvamukta, Hastivarman of Veṅgi, Ugrasêna of Palakka, Kubêra who reigned in Dêvarâshṭra and Dhanañjaya whose capital was Kosthalapura. Samudra-Gupta being repulsed by the kings of the Eastern Deccan, abandoned the conquests he had made in the coast of Orissa and returned home.

Of all the kings mentioned in the Allâhâbàd inscription, there is only one who is known in other ways; it is Vishṇugòpa of Kâñchi whose name figures in the Vâyalûr inscription (see The Pallavas" pages 20 and 23).

§ 3. The Pallavas from 340 to 610 A. D.

We now propose to study the history of the kings who have reigned after Vishṇugôpa, the adversary of Samudra-Gupta about 340 A. D., up to Mahêndravarman I, the adversary of Pulakêśin II. about 610 A. D.

In chapter II of my work "The Pallavas", I have shown that the Vâyalûr inscription enables us to construct the following genealogy :

Kumâravishṇu
|
Skandavarman
|
Viravarman
|
Skandavarman
|
— Siṁhavarman
  |
  Skandavarman
  |
  Nandivarman
— Yuvamahârâja Vishṇugôpa
  |
  Siṁhavarman
  |
  Vishṇugôpa
  |
  Siṁhavarman
  |
  Siṁhavishṇu
  |
  Mahêndravarman I.

In fact, the Ôṁgôḍu No. 1 plates (G. O. No. 99, 29th Aug. 1916, Part II, No. 3), Ôṁgôḍu No. 2 (G. O. No. 99, 29th Aug. 1916, Part II, No. 4), Pikira (Ep. Ind., Vol VIII, p. 159,) Mâṅgaḷûr (Ind. Ant., Vol. V, page 154) and Chûra (G. O. No. 920, 4th Aug. 1914, Part II, No. 1) give us the following genealogy :

Kumâravishnu
|
Skandavarman
|
Viravarman
|
Skandavarman
|
Yuvamahârâja Vishṇugôpa
|
Siṁhavarman
|
Vishṇugôpa.

It must be noted that the Chûra plates which are dated in the reign of the last king give him for grandfather Vishṇugôpa with the title of Mahârâja, whereas the other documents call him Yuvamahârâja. This detail is of very little importance, for the documents sometimes give us incorrect details about the grandfather of a reigning sovereign. This genealogy can therefore be accepted with certainty.

The copper plates of Uruvupalli (Ind. Ant. Vol. V, page 20) give us the succession : Skandavarman, Viravarman, Skandavarman, Yuvamahârâja Vishṇugôpa, which conforms absolutely to the one given above; but these plates are dated in the reign of a king named Siṁhavarman whose relationship to the other kings is not given. The most natural supposition would be to take this Siṁhavarman to be the elder brother of Yuvamahârâja Vishṇugôpa and consequently the son of Skandavarman. The Udayêndiram plates (Ep. Ind. Vol III, p. 142) give the following genealogy :

Skandavarman
|
Siṁhavarman
|
Skandavarman
|
Nandivarman

in which we find a Siṁhavarman, son of a Skandavarman. One may therefore be tempted to believe that the Siṁhavarman of the Udayendiram plates was the grandson of Viravarman.

The Vayâlûr inscription (see "The Pallavas", chapter II) has thrown a final solution on this problem since it gives us the following series :

(23) Vîravarman,
(24) Skandavarman,
(25) Simhavarman,
(26) Skandavarman,
(27) Nandivarman.

The Vêlûrpâlaiyam plates (South Indian Inscriptions, Vol. II., Part V, give us a brief history of the Pallavas of Kâñchî ; after having spoken, in verse 9, of Nandivarman, these plates say: " Then from the king named Simhavarman...was born the victorious Simhavishṇu". According to this passage it would appear that Simhavarman, the father of Simhavishṇu was the successor but not the son of Nandivarman, because we have here "then" and not "from him" and this supposition has been completely confirmed by the Vâyalûr inscription which gives the following series :

(29) Simhavarman,
(30) Vishṇugôpa,
(31) Simhavarman,
(32) Simhavishṇu,
(33) Mahêndravarman (I).

Thus it follows that Simhavishṇu was the grandson of Vishṇugôpa of the Chûra plates. Indeed, in the Vâyalûr inscription, as well as in the Chûra plates, this Vishṇugôpa figures as the son and successor of a king named Simhavarman.

So then, in my opinion, the genealogy I have given at the beginning of this chapter can be considered as correct.

We have thus utilised all the documents that we have, with the exception only of the Chendalûr plates (Ep. Ind. Vol. VIII, page 233), which give the following genealogy :

Skandavarman
|
Kumâravishṇu (I.)
|
Buddhavarman
|
Kumâravishṇu (II.) king of Kâñchi.

Up to this time, all the authors that have tried to connect

this genealogy with the one that we just examined have completely failed. I humbly confess that the theory I have propounded in my work "The Pallavas" pages 17 and 22 is entirely "untenable." I have supposed that these plates were a copy of a document dated at the beginning of the IV century. I now admit that this is not possible, for if the text of these plates belonged to circ. 300 A.D., it will probably be in Prâkṛit; but the Chendalûr plates are in Sanskṛit and their phraseology clearly points to the middle of the V century, that is to say, circ. 450 A.D.

Recently I made a special study of this question and these are the results I have arrived at:

(1) There is so great a resemblance between the phraseology of the Chendalûr plates and those of Uruvupalli that there can be no doubt that the two grants were nearly contemporaneous. Professor Hultzsh has remarked that whole sentences were common to both these documents.

(2) From a palæographic point of view, Professor Hultzsh has compared the alphabet of the Chendalûr plates and those of Uruvupalli, Mâṅgalûr, Pikira and has established that the letters "ra" and "ka" seemed to be more developed in the Chendalûr document and that it must therefore be more modern. When I myself examined the alphabet of these four documents, I observed that, if the letters "ra" and "ka" were in fact developed a little more, there were as a set-off other letters such as "ha," "ya," etc, which were developed a little less and that all that one can say on comparing the letters individually is that the Chendalûr document was contemporaneous with the other three.

But, if, instead of comparing the letters, we compare the general aspect of the writings, the Chendalûr plates appear to be a little irregular and disorderly which is a characteristic of the ancient documents, whereas, the plates of Uruvupalli, Mâṇgaḷûr, Pikira possess the order and regularity that belong to more modern writings. However, I do not believe that, in general, a comparison of the alphabets can give us any very correct information. Not only the plates of the Pallavas but also those of the Gaṅgas and the Kadambas prove that the alphabets differ much according to the scribes who have engraved the plates; and the documents of the same reign do not sometimes resemble one another. Lastly, I think that there is no need to compare the Chendalûr plates dated from Kâñchîpuram with those of Uruvupalli dated from Palakkada, Mâṅgaḷûr dated from Daśanapura, and Pikira dated from Mênmatura: the towns of Palakkada, Daśanapura and Mênmatura were probably in the Guṇṭur district, that is, far away from Kâñchîpuram and the difference of the countries fully explains the difference in the alphabets.

(3) We have said that the Chendalûr plates were surely almost contemporaneous with those of Uruvupalli and we have also pointed out that the alphabet of the plates does not enable us to say if Kumâravishṇu II. of Chandalûr who reigned in Kâñchî was the predecessor or successor of Siṁhavarman of Uruvupalli who probably reigned at Kâñchî while his brother the Yuvamahârâja Vishṇugôpa reigned over the province of Palakkada. Now we shall find that it is certain that Kumâravishṇu II. did not reign after Siṁhavarman. In fact, the grand-son of the latter, Nandivarman, reigned at Kâñchî (Udayendiram plates) and we learn from the grant of Vêlûrpâḷaiyam that Nandivarman had for successors Siṁhavarman and Siṁhavishṇu who was surely reigning at Kâñchî because he conquered the Chôḷa kingdom; after Siṁhavarman, we cannot find a place for the dynasty of Chendalûr. Besides, the Vâyalûr inscription places the series Skandavarman-Kumâravishṇu-Buddhavarman before the series Siṁhavarman-Skandavarman-Nandivarman; and the Vêlûrpâḷaiyam plates place Kumarâvishṇu and Buddhavarman (mentioned in verse 8) before Vishṇugôpa and Nandivarman (mentioned in verse 9).

There is therefore room to think that the series of kings:

Skandavarman

|

Kumâravishṇu (I.)

|

Buddhavarman

|

Kumâravishṇu (II.)
(the donor of the Chendalur plates)

have reigned at Kâñchi before the series :

Simhavarman
(mentioned in the Uruvupalli plates)
|
Skandavarman
|
Nandivarman,

and owing to the resemblance between the Chendalûr and Uruvupalli plates, Kumâravishṇu II would have been the immediate predecessor of Simhavarman at Kâñchî.

At the end of 1915, Mr. C. R. Krishnamachari, Telugu Assistant in the Epigraphical Office of Madras, has made a discovery which I consider to be of very great importance for the history of the Pallavas, I mean the discovery of the Ômgôdu No. 1 plates (Report on Epigraphy, G.O. No. 99, 29th Aug. 1916; Part. II., page 113) which gives us the following genealogy :

Kumâravishṇu
|
Skandavarman
|
Viravarmam
|
Skandavarman.

We must note, first of all, that the last of these kings did not probably reign at Kâñchi since the document is dated from Tâmbrâpa. Who then reigned at Kâñchi when Skandavarman reigned in the Guṇṭûr district ? As this Skandavarman is the father of Simhavarman and the Yuvamahârâja Vishnugôpa of the Uruvupalli plates, we may suppose that the king who reigned at the time of Viravarman and Skandavarman of Ômgôḍu No. 1 was Kumâravishṇu II of Chendalûr.

But there is something more : the Ômgôḍu No. 1 plates mention a king called Kumâravishṇu, a name which we find mentioned twice in the Chendalûr genealogy ; but since Kumâravishṇu II. probably reigned at the time of Viravarman and his son Skanda, it is Kumâravishṇu I. who can be identified with the one of Ômgôḍu No. 1.

So we obtain the following genealogy which agrees with all the documents that we possess :

Skandavarman (350-375 A. D.)
|
Kumâravishṇu I. (375-400 A. D.)
|
- Buddhavarman
  |
  Kumâravishṇu II.
  (King of Kâñchi)
- Skandavarman (400-425 A. D.)
  |
  Viravarman (425-450 A. D.)
  |
  Skandavarman (450-475 A. D.)
  |
  - Siṁhavarman
    (King of Kâñchi)
    |
    Skandavarman
    |
    Nandivarman
    (King of Kâñchi)
  - Y. Vishṇugôpa (475-500 A. D.)
    (Governor of Palakkada.)
    |
    Siṁhavarman (500-525 A. D.)
    |
    Vishṇugôpavarman (525-550 A. D.)
    (King of Palakkada)
    |
    Siṁhavarman (550-575 A. D.)
    |
    Siṁhavishṇu (575-600 A. D.)
    (King of Kâñchi)
    |
    Mahêndravarman I. (600-625 A. D.)

It is to be observed that in the Ôṁgôḍu No. 1 plates the name of Viravarman is not preceded by any title. It is therefore probable that he did not reign but died young: so that Kumâravishṇu II of Kâñchi was the contemporary of Skandavarman of Taṁbrâpa and the immediate predecessor, at Kâñchi, of Siṁhavarman.

In the chronology given above, we have admitted that Mahêndravarman I. ascended the throne about 600 A. D. and we have allowed for each generation an average of 25 years.

It is probable that the first of these kings, Skandavarman (350-375), was the son and successor of Vishṇugôpa of Kâñchi who reigned there from 325 to 350 at the time of Samudra-Gupta.

It is more easy for us to construct the genealogy of these

kings than to compile their history, because the copper-plates give us always the names of the great-grandfather, the grandfather and the father of the donor, but these names are not followed by any historical details. They have words of praise added to them which are purely conventional and are applied indiscriminately in a haphazard manner to any king.

The only thing we know is that from 400 A.D. to 550 A.D. the empire remained always divided into two kingdoms: Toṇḍaimaṇḍalam in the south with Kâñchi for its capital and the present districts of Guṇṭûr and Nellore in the north with Tâmbrâpa, Palakkada, Menmaturâ and Daśanapura for capitals.

We can also have some additional information when we proceed to study the Gaṅgas and the Kadambas.

From the time of Siṁhavishṇu the history of the Pallavas becomes clear. I think it is useless to repeat here what I have said in my book "The Pallavas," page 36; I shall be content with saying here again that Siṁhavishṇu vanquished the Malaya, Kaḷabhra, Mâlava, Chôḷa, Pâṇḍya and Siṁhala king and the Kêraḷas, conquered the Chôḷa kingdom and took possession of the banks of the Kâvêri; that Mahêndra was pursued by Pulakêśin II. up to the banks of the Kâvêri, that he succeeded in defeating his adversary at the battle of Pullalûr and preserved the country of Kâñchi; but he lost the districts of Guṇṭûr and Nellore which remained in the hands of the Châḷukyas.

Concerning the Pallava civilisation at the time of Mahêndravarman I., I request the reader to refer to the following works:

Concerning Architecture: "Mahêndravarman inscription at Conjeeveram," Pondicherry 1919.

Concerning Sculpture: "Pallava Antiquities" Vol. I. Chapter II.

Concerning Drama: "The Mattavilâsaprahasana;" Trivandram Sanskrit Series No. L V.

Concerning Poesy and Music: "The Pallavas" page 39.

Concerning Painting and Dance: "My forthcoming paper entitled "Pallava painting," concerning the fresco-paintings at Śittaṇṇâvâśal.

GENEALOGY OF THE PALLAVAS

"Bappa-dêva" (225-250)
Skandavarman (250-275)
Buddhavarman (275-300)
[Buddhyaṅ]kura (300-325).
Vishṇugôpa (325-350)
Skandavarman (350-375)
Kumâravishṇu I (375-400)

- Buddhavarman (400-425)
  - Kumâravishṇu II (425-450)
- Skandavarman
  - Vîravarman
  - Skandavarman (450-475)

- Siṁhavarman (475-500)
  - Skandavarman (500-525)
  - Nandivarman I (525-550)
- Yuvamahârâja Vishṇugôpa
  - Siṁhavarman
  - Vishṇugôpa
  - Siṁhavarman (550-575)

- Siṁhavishṇu (575-600)
  - Mahêndravarman I (600-630)
  - Narasiṁhavarman I (630-668)
  - Mahêndravarman II (668-670)
  - Paramêśvaravarman I (670-690)
  - Narasiṁhavarman II (690-715)
  - Paramêśvaravarman II (715-717)
- Bhimavarman
  - Buddhavarman
  - Âdityavarman
  - Gôvindavarman
  - Hiraṇyavarman
  - Nandivarman II (717-779)
  - Dantivarman (779-830)
  - Nandivarman III (830-854)
  - Nṛipatuṅga (854-880)
  - Aparâjita (880-900)

CHAPTER IV.

THE DYNASTIES OF CENTRAL DECCAN.

§ 1. The Vâkâṭakas.

Till now, no one has thought of classing the Vâkâṭakas among the dynasties of Deccan; it was believed that it was a dynasty that had to be studied with the dynasties of the North. An example of this error is given by Kielhorn who classes the Vâkâṭaka inscriptions (nos. 618 to 624) under the rubric "Inscriptions of Northern India".

Now then, I wish to make the following declaration: when trying to compile the ancient history of the Deccan, I have come to the conclusion that the Vâkâṭakas must be classed among the dynasties of the Deccan; and what is more, I can affirm that, of all the dynasties of the Deccan that have reigned from the III to be VI century, the most glorious, the most important, the one that must be given the place of honour, the one that has excelled all others, the one that has had the greatest influence on the civilisation of the whole of the Deccan, is unquestionably the illustrious dynasty of the Vâkâṭakas.

The undermentioned documents: Chammak (Gupta Inscriptions, No. 55, p. 235), Siwanî (Gup'a Inscriptions, No. 56 p. 243), Dudia (Ep. Ind., Vol III, p. 258), Bâlâghât (Ep. Ind., Vol. IX, p. 268), Professor K. B. Pâthak's plates (Ind. Ant., Vol. XLI, 1912, p. 215), two inscriptions at Ajaṇṭâ (A. S. W. I. IV, pp. 53, 124 and 129), and the inscription in the Ghaṭotkacha cave at Guwârâ (A. S. W. I., vol IX, pp. 64 and 138) give us the following genealogy :

Vindyaśakti
|
Pravarasêna I.
|
Gautamiputra
|
Rudrasêna I.
|
Pṛithivishêṇa I.
|
Rudrasêna II.
|
Pravarasêna II.
|
a son — Dêvasêna — Harishêṇa
Narêndrasêna — Pṛithivishêṇa II.

The first Mahârâja, Pravarasêna I. was the son of Vindyaśakti, "the banner of the Vâkâṭaka race" mentioned in the Ajaṇṭâ (A. S. W. I., IV, p. 124) inscription without any royal title. Pravarasêna I. performed sacrifices, especially Aśvamedha. Gautamîputra, who died probably before his father, as is seen by his never being a Mahârâja, married the daughter of Bhavanâga, king of the Bhâraśivas, "who were besprinkled on the forehead with the pure water of Bhâgîrathî (the Gaṅgâ)". It is probable that Bhavanâga who reigned near the Ganges belonged to the family of the Nâgas of Padmâvati.

We know nothing about Rudrasêna I. His son Pṛithivishena reigned for a long time. Mr. Vincent A. Smith attributes an inscription (Gupta Inscriptions, No. 53 and 54, page 233) at Nâchnâ to this king; but when writing, Mr. Vicent A. Smith has not taken into account the Bâlâghat plates which show that there was a second Pṛithivishêṇa. Is the Nâchnâ stone dated in the time of Pṛithivishêṇa I. or Pṛithivishêṇa II ? Judging from the form of the letters I would attribute it rather to the second ; the small circle at the head of the letters seems to point rather to the V than to the IV century [for the History of the Vâkâṭakas by Mr. Vincent A. Smith, see J. R. A. S.; April 1914, page 317].

The 8th verse of the Ajaṇṭâ inscription says that Pṛithivishêṇa I. vanquished the king of Kuntaḷa, i. e, the Kadamba king.

The passage that follows it is so badly damaged that we can read nothing therein. The name of Rudrasêna II. is not visible; but it is not probable it has been omitted. In fact, this prince had the honour of marrying Prabhâvatî, daughter of Chandra-Gupta II. the illustrious emperor of the Gupta dynasty. Mr. Vincent A. Smith (J. R. A. S.; 1914, p. 326) thinks that this marriage took place about 395 A. D. and we shall admit this date. It was at this time that Chandra-Gupta II. took possession of the kingdom of the Western Satrapas, and it is certain that the Vâkâṭaka empire adjoined that of the Western Satrapas; and the conclusion of Mr. Vincent A. Smith, which is very important for the chronology of the dynasty, is probably the right one.

Professor K. B. Pâthak's plates (Ind. Ant., 1912, page 215) is a grant of land issued by Queen Prabhâvatî, widow of Rudrasêna II, during the minority of her son the Yuvarâja Divakârasena. It seems therefore that Rudrasêna II. died shortly after his marriage and that about the year 400 A. D. the queen Prabhâvatî, the glorious daughter of the Gupta emperor was the regent of the Vâkâṭaka kingdom. We have said that Prithivishêṇa I. vanquished the king of Kuntaḷa; and Kuntaḷa is the empire of the Kadambas: the town of Halsi, in Belgaum district, which was at one time called Palâśikâ (Halasige) was originally in the Kuntaḷa kingdom (Ep. Ind. Vol XIII., p. 299; Kadamba inscription, verses 58-62). The Vâkâṭakas were the neigbours of the Kadambas and the Vâkâṭaka kingdom extended up to the modern town of Kurnool on the banks of the Kṛishṇâ. We know that the famous temple of Śrîśailam or Śrî-Parvata is in the Kurnool district; and a "story, as related " in the Sthala Mâhâtmya of the place, says that the princess " Chandravatî, a daughter of the Gupta king Chandragupta " conceived a passion for the God on the Śriśaila hill and " began offering every day a garland of jasamine (mallikâ) " flowers to him" (Report on Epigraphy for 1914-1915-G. O.

No. 1260, 25th Aug. 1915, Part II, No. 13, page 91). This information is very precious as throwing light on the origin of the dynasty of the Vishṇukuṇḍins that we shall study further. In fact, we shall see that this dynasty had for its tutelary deity, the God of Śrî-Parvata; and that the first king of this dynasty, Mâdhavavarman married a Vishṇukuṇḍin princess. I think there can be no doubt that this princess was the daughter or the grand daughter of queen Prâbhâvatî or Chandravati who was the daughter of the Gupta emperor, wife of Rudrasêna II. mother of Pravarasêna II. and a votary of the God of Śrî-Parvata. It is probably during the reign of Pravarasêna II. that the Vâkâṭakas who reigned over almost the whole of the modern State of Hayderabad, succeeded in founding the dynasty of the Vishṇukuṇḍins by placing on the throne of Vêṅgî, Mâdhavavarman I who was the husband of a Vâkâṭaka princess and an adorer of the God of Śrî-Parvata.

We do not know if the Yuvarâja Divakârasêna ascended the throne. We only know for certain that a son of Rudrasêna II. reigned under the name Pravarasêna II. The poet Bana in his introduction to Harshacharita mentions, among the most famous poets that had preceeded him, Pravarasêna who was the author of a work called Sêtukavya. The capital of Pravarasêna was called Pravarapura and was probably founded by that king. It is certain that Pravarasêna II. reigned in the south of Jabalpur (Jubbulpore) in the country in which we now find the towns of Seuni (Seoni) and Elichpur (Ilichpur). The Narbadâ separated his kingdom from that of the Guptas. Chammak (Charmâṅka) is situated on the banks of Mahânadî Gupta Insc., page 241). We have said that the Vâkâṭka empire extended further south. In 450 A. D. the Vâkâṭaka empire had the following boundaries : in the north it was separated by the Narbadâ from the kingdom of Ujjain where reigned the illustrious emperor Kumâra-Gupta I. In the east was the vassal state of Raypur of which we shall speak further : the king Mahâ-Sudêva had Śarabhapura for his capital. In the south-east was situated the kingdom of the Vishṇukuṇḍins over which Mâdhavavarman I was reigning at Vêṅgî. In the south west, the river Bhîmâ separated the Vâkâṭakas empire from that of the Kâdambas whose king Śântivarman was the " master of the entire Karṇṇâta region";

one of his capitals was Palâsikâ (Halsi in Belgaum). In the west the Traikûṭas occupied the coast province of Aparânta. Thus the Vâkâṭakas reigned over on empire that occupied a very central position and it is through this dynasty that the high civilisation of the Gupta empire and the Sanskṛit culture in particular spread throughout the Deccan. Between 400 A. D. and 500 A. D. the Vâkâṭâkas occupied a predominant position and we may say that *"In the history of the Deccan the V century is the century of the Vâkâtakas"*.

The alphabet of the plates of this dynasty is very peculiar: it is "box-headed". We shall have occasion to revert to this subject when speaking of the Kadambas.

According to the Ajaṇṭâ inscription, the son of Pravarasêna II, whose name has been lost, must have ascended the throne when he was 8 years old (Arch. Surv. West. Ind., Vol. IV., page 125) It is probable that this prince was dethroned by his younger brother Nârendrasêna. In fact, the Bâlâghat plates say that Narêndrasêna "appropriated or took away the family's fortune." Narêndrasêna was married to Ajjhitabhaṭṭârikâ, daughter of the king of Kuntaḷa. This marriage took place probably about 445 A. D. We have admitted that Rudrasêna II married the daughter of Chandra-Gupta II about 395 A. D. It is probable that the marriage of the grandson took place about 50 years after; we shall see later on that this king of Kuntaḷa was probably the Kadamba Kakusthavarman. The Bâlâghat plates say about Narêndrasêna that "his commands were honoured by the lords of Kôsala, Mèkala and Mâlava, and he held in check enemies bowed down by his prowess" This latter event took place after 467 A. D. It is impossible that Narèndrasêna should be able to give orders to the Mâlava king before this date: in fact, from 455 to 467 A. D., the king of Ujjain was the illustrious Skanda-Gupta Vikramâditya (Mr. Panna Lall in "The dates of Skanda-Gupta and his successors," Hindustan Review, Jan. 1918, argues that the reign of Skanda-Gupta ended about A. D. 467. See also, "Annals of the Bhandarkar institute 1918-19, Vol. I, Part I, page 69). From 484 to 494 A. D. the country situated between the Jamnâ and the Narmadâ was under the orders of Budha-Gupta.

Pṛithivishêṇa II, son of Narêndrasêna, was reigning at the time when the Bâlâghât plates were engraved.

It is impossible to know if Dêvasêna reigned at the same time as Pṛithivishêṇa II or after ; it was probably at the end of the V century. The minister of Dêvasêna was Hastibhoja who probably dug the Ghaṭotkacha cave at Gulwârâ, eleven miles W. of Ajaṇṭâ.

Harishêṇa, son of Dêvasêna reigned probably about 500 to 530 A. D. It is probable that this king made conquests in all directions, since the Ajaṇṭâ inscription mentions Kuntaḷa (the Kadamba kingdom) Avanti (Mâḷwà), Kaliṅga, Kosala, Trikûṭa, Lâṭa and Ândhra. These évents probably took place from 500 to 515 A. D. In fact it is about 500 A. D. that Râvivarman killed Srî-Vishṇuvarman, who was reigning at Pâlâśikâ ; Harivarman might have contributed to the struggle against the king of Kuntaḷa. In the VI century we have not a single document of the Traikûṭas. It is therefore probable that they were destroyed by Harishêṇa at the begniming of this century. It is also probable that it was at the beginning of the VI century that Indra of Kaliṅga fought with Indra the Vishṇukuṇḍin ; and possibly Harishêṇa had to interfere in the affairs of the Kaliṇga and the Ândhra (between the Gôdâvârî and the Kṛishṇâ). Again, an inscription of Eran (Gupta Insc., p.93), dated 510-511 mentions a fight in which Bhânu-Gupta was allied with the king of Śarabha i.e. the king of Kosala. It is perhaps at this time that Harishêṇa fought with the kings of Avanti (Mâḷwâ) and Mêkala (the Narbadâ).

It is probable that the Vâkâṭaka dynasty was replaced, in the middle of the VI century, by that of the Kaḷachuris who held possession of all the country between Nâsik and Ujjain in the second half of the VI century.

§ 2. The kings of Śarabhapura.

The seal of the Khariar plates (Ep. Ind. Vol. IX, page 171) bears the following genealogy :

Prasanna
|
Mânamâtra
|
Mahâ Sudêva

Dr. Von Konow in editing these plates, has observed that the word Mânamâtra was synonymous with Mânaṅka, the words Màtra and Aṅka meaning "ornament," and the Uṇḍivâṭika plates give us the following genealogy (Ep. Ind. Vol. VIII, p. 163 and Ind. Ant. Vol. XXX):

Mânâṅka
|
Dêvarâja
|
Bhavishya
|
Abhimanyu.

The king Dêvarâja had many sons of whom Bhavishya was one. Abhimanyu resided at Mânapuram (Mâna-town) which is identified with Mânpur (lat. 23°46' ; long. 81°11' E ; see Gupta Inscriptions, page 136) near Bandhogarh in Rêwa. The Uṇḍivâṭika plates were issued to make a grant to the temple of [Pêṭha]- Paṅgaraka which has been identified with Pagara near Pachmarhî (Sohagpur Tahśil ; Hoshangabad Dist ; Central Provinces). The king Mânaṅka is described as being "the ornament of the Rashṭrakûṭas." We have thus the two following series :

(Khariar plates)	*(Undivâtika plates)*
Mânamâtra	Mânanka
|	|
Mahâ Sudêva	Dêvarâja

Three documents, the Khariar (Ep. Ind., Vol. IX; page 170) Raipur (Gupta Inscriptions, page 196) and Sârangarh (Ep. Ind., Vol IX, page 281) copper plates, speak of king Sudêva (Mahâ-Sudêva-râja) who had Śarabhapura for his capital ; this town cannot be identified ; however, it is probable that this king reigned in the neighbourhood of the modern town of Raypur which is situated to the south of the Mahânadi and near its source. This kingdom was therefore situated between Kaliṅga in the east and the kingdom of the Vâkâṭakas in the west. It is also very probable that the kings of Śarabhapura were the vassals of the Vâkâṭakas.

It is also from Śarabhapura that were issued the Arang plates (Gupta Inscriptions, page 191) which speak of the king Jaya (Jayarâja). This king was almost the contemporary of Sudêva, since the alphabets resemble each other. However it is impossible to know the relationship that existed between these two princes.

The alphabet of the plates issued from Śarabhapura has a peculiar characteristic ; it is box-headed as in the Siwani plates (Gupta Inscriptions, page 243) which are dated in the reign of Pravarasêna II.

I believe we can place the two kings Sudêva and Jaya approximately in the second half of the V century.

It is possible that their kingdom was the Southern Kôsala.

An inscription of Eran (Gupta Inscriptions, page 93) gives us the following genealogy :

...............râja

|

Mâdhava

who married the daughter of the king of Śarabha,

|

Gôparâja

who was the ally of Bhânu-Gupta and was killed a little before the year 510-511 A. D.

To sum up, we know very little about this dynasty. However, we may suppose—it is only a hypothesis—that the genealogy was as follows ;

Prasanna
(of the Rashṭrakûṭa family)
|
Mânamâtra
(king of Mânapura)
|
Su-dêva-râja
|
Jayarâja (king of Śarabha) | Bhavishya
|
Abhimanyu
(king of Mânapura)

Jayarâja was perhaps the son of Sudêva, as the Uṇḍivâtika plates say that Dêvarâja had many sons and it therefore appears that Bhavishya was not the eldest.

CHAPTER V.

THE DYNASTIES OF WESTERN DECCAN.

§ 1. The Âbhîras.

At the end of the II century and the first half of the III century the Âbhîras were powerful in Gujarât and Kâṭhiâwar. An inscription (Ind. Ant. Vol X., page 157) of the Western Kshatrapas dated 181 A.D. (Ś. 103) is a donation by general (senâpati) Rudrabhûti, who was an Âbhîra and the son of general Bâhaka. In Mâḷwâ, in Gujarât and in Kâṭhiâwar have been found silver coins of a king named Iśvaradatta. Mr. Rapson (page CXXXVI) says: "there can be little doubt then that Iśvaradatta reigned some time between A. D. 236 and A. D. 239." Besides, it seems that the power of the Western Kshatrapas began to decline at this epoch: "Already in this reign (of Vijayasêna) appear the first symptoms of a decline about the year 167 or 168 (A. D.245-246)" (Rapson, page 137). At Nâsik (Ep. Ind. Vol. VIII., page 88) there is an inscription (No. 1137 of Lüders's list) dated in the 9th year of Mâḍharîputra Iśvarasêna, an Âbhîra, son of Śivadatta. The latter is not mentioned as being a king. It would therefore appear that Iśvarasêna founded the Âbhîra dynasty.

Is this Âbhîra named Iśvarasêna the same as the king Iśvaradatta of the coins, who, towards the middle of the III century founded the Âbhîra dynasty and carved out for himself a kingdom extending over Kâṭhiâwar and the Nâsik region?

§ 3, The Traikûṭas,

This dynasty (see Rapson, sections 42, 132, 134) reigned on the coast north of Bombay.

They have found (J. B. B. R. A. S., 1914, Vol. XXIII., pages 1 to 7) some coins that mention a certain king named Indradatta and his son Dahragaṇa, some other coins that mention a king called Indradatta and his son Daharasêna and a few others that mention Dahragaṇa and his son Vyâghragaṇa.

The Pardi plates (J. B. B. R. A. S., Vol XVI, Art. XIX; page 346) are dated in the reign of Dahrasêna and in the 207th year of the era used by the Traikûṭas.

The Surat plates (Ep. Ind., Vol XI, page 219) are dated in the reign of Vyaghrasêna in the year 241 and the plates discovered at Kaṇhêri by Mr. Bird are dated in the year 245.

It is admitted that the era used by the Traikûṭas is nothing but the Kaḷachuri or Chêdi era which begins on the 5th September 248 A.D. (Ep. Ind., Vol IX, page 129). So Dahrasêna reigned in 455-6 A.D; Vyaghrasêna in 489-90 and the Kaṇhêri plates are dated in the year 493-494 A.D. It is quite possible that this era was not founded by the Traikûtas; it was perhaps founded by the Âbhiras.

A close examination of these documents enables us to admit that the kings whose name ends in "gaṇa" may be identified with those whose name ends in "sêna"

Thus we have the following genealogy:

Indradatta
|
Dahrasêna (who reigned in 455 A.D.)
|
Vyaghrasêna (who reigned in 490 A.D.)

The Traikûṭa is mentioned by Kâlidâsa.

The Vâkâṭaka Harisheṇa conquered it.

The Pardi plates have been issued from the town of Âmrakâ and the Surat plates from Aniruddhapura.

§ 4. The Kaḷachuris.

The Abhona plates (Ep. Ind. Vol VI., page 294) and Sarsavni plates (Ep. Ind., Vol. VI., page 295) give us the following genealogy :

Kṛishṇarâja
|
Śaṁkaragaṇa (who reigned in 595 A.D.)
|
Buddharâja (who reigned in 610 A.D.)

These kings use the special era we have already spoken of.

We have a coin of Kṛishṇarâja (Prog. Rep. Arch. Surv. West. Ind. for 1914-15, page 60).

It seems that the reign of Śaṁkaragaṇa was glorious : the Abhona plates tell us that he had his capital at Ujjain and reigned over the Nâsik regions which denotes a vast empire.

The chief Nirihullaka reigned in the lower Narbadâ valley about 580 A. D., and was a feudatory (Sânkhîḍa grant; Ep. Ind., Vol. II., page 22) of Śaṁkaragana. Nirihullaka was perhaps a descendant of Saṁgamasiṁha who was king of Barakuchchha in 292 i. e. 530-531 A. D. (Sunao-Kala plates).

Buddharâja probably met with great reverses : before the year A.D. 601 (Bâdâmi inscription) the king Maṇgalêśa of the Chaḷukya dynasty vanquished him. In 609 A.D. he reigned at Vidiśa (Bêsnagar, near Bhilsâ, Vadner plates). In 610 A.D. (Sarsavni plates) he reigned at Ânandapura (Ânand in Kaira dist.; Ep. Ind., Vol. VI., page 297) and gave orders about the Barukachcha-vishaya.

We know (Aihole inscription) that Pulakêśin II vanquished Lâta, Gujarat and Mâḷwa.

CHAPTER VI.

THE DYNASTIES OF EASTERN DECCAN.

§ 1.—The Ikshvâkus.

Three inscriptions (Ind, Ant., Vol XI, page 256) found ("Amarâvati and Jagayyapêta Stûpa", Arch. Surv. Southern India, page 110) on the ruins of the stûpa at Jagayyapêta (Nandigâma Taluk, Krishṇâ district) give the name of a king called Mâḍhariputra Śrî Vira Purushadatta (Purisadata) of the Ikshvâkus (Ikhâkus) and are in an alphabet which seems to point to the III century of the Christan era.

What became of this dynasty later on, it is impossible to say. However, there exists a stone in Guḍḍappa dry land at Aṇaji in the Dâvaṇagere taluq of Mysore (Ep. Carn., Vol. XI, Dg, No. 161) which mentions "the family of the Kèkayas, who made intermarriages with the Ikshvâkus."

§ 2. The Bṛihatphalâyanas.

The Koṇḍamudi plates (Ep. Ind., Vol. VI., p. 315) are dated in the 10th year of king Jayavarman, of the Bṛihatphalâyanas, who reigned at Kudûra. The alphabet of these plates is extremely archaic; they are in prâkṛit; besides, "the language and phraseology of the inscription are so similar to the Nâsik inscriptions of Gautamîputra Śâtakarṇi and of Vâsishthîputra Puḷumâyi, that Jayavarman's date cannot have been very distant from that of those two Ândhra kings" (Ep. Ind Vol. VII, No. 31, page 315). It must however be noted that the legend on the seal is in Sanskṛit. It is therefore certain that Jayavarman reigned immediately after the Śâtavâhanas.

The Koṇḍamudi plates record the grant of the village of Pâṇṭûra in Kudûrahâra which is the province, as we know, of which Kudûra was the capital. Where were this province and especially this town of Kudûra situated ? Koṇḍamudi, where the plates have been found, is situated in the Tenali taluq which is not far from the mouth of the Kṛishṇâ. The town of Kudûra is found mentioned in an inscription at Amarâvati (No. 1295 of Lüders's list). The country of Kuduhâra or Kudrahâra is mentioned in the plates of Nandivarman of the Śâlaṅkâyana dynasty. These plates were issued from Vengî and have been found near the Kolleru lake (Ind. Ant., Vol V, 1876, page 175. See also Burnell, "South Indian Palægraphy, 2e Ed. page 135.) The country called Kudrahâra or Guḍrahara is referred to in many documents (see in particular : Ind. Ant., Vol XIII, page 138, line 17; Ind. Ant., Vol VII, page 191, line 12, and the Reṇḍubaḷḷi copper-plate, Rep. on Epigraphy for 1914-1915, G. O. No. 1260, Public, 25th Aug. 1915, page 8, copper-plate No. 2 of 1915) The geographical indications given by these documents [see also : Ind. Ant., Vol VIII, page 76; S. I. I. Vol I, page 47; and inscriptions Nos 539 and 544 of 1893) show that Kudûrahâra or Guḍrahâra is the country adjoining the modern town of Masulipatam (Bandar.)

Besides, there have been found at Masulipatam (Bandar Taluk) four sets of copper-plates that give information about this country :

(1) The grant of Amma II. (S. I. I., Vol I., page 47) containing an order to the people living in Gudravâra-vishaya.

(2) The plates of Vijayâditya III. (Ind. Ant., Vol. XX, page 103, and Ep. Ind., Vol. V., page 122) granting the village of Tranḍapâru situated in the Guḍravâra-vishaya.

(3) The plates of Bhima II. (Ind. Ant., Vol. XX., page 270, and Ep. Ind., Vol. V., page 135) granting a field in Guḍravâra-vishaya.

(4) The plates of Amma II. (Ind. Ant., Vol. VIII, page 74 ; and Vol. XX, p. 271 ; Ep. Ind., Vol. V., page 139) granting land. The last document is interesting as it shows the precise position of the land : it was situated beside the village of Pâmbaṟṟu in the Guḍravâra-vishaya and near Ghaṇṭaśâlâ ; again this grant of land was made to a chief "for having improved the town of Gudrâvâra" ; we know that Ghaṇṭaśâlâ, which was situated in Gudravâra-vishaya is a village in the Divi taluq situated at a distance of 10 miles from Masulipatam (Bandar) and 6 miles from the village of Kûdûru.

We shall therefore conclude that the town of Kudûra, which was the capital of Jayavarman in the III century of the Christian era, is but the modern village which is 4 miles west-north-west of Masulipatam and 6 miles from the village of Ganṭhaśâla and is mentioned under the name of Kûdûru (Z) in the list of villages of Bandar (Masulipatam) taluq (see "List of villages of the Madras Presidency," 1914, page 150). The village named Pâṇṭura in the Konḍamudi plates, is perhaps Panduru, a village in the Bandar (Masulipatam) taluq.

It so happens that the result we have arrived at is found to be of immense importance not only for the ancient history of the Deccan but also of Indo-China.

We know that the civilisation of Indo-China is of Indian origin and a study of the Indo-Chinese documents has proved that the civilisation of Indo-China came almost exclusively from the Deccan. The Indo-Chinese inscriptions are dated in the Ṣaka era and their alphabets very closely resemble those of the inscriptions in the Deccan. Such an inscription of Cambodia (see, "Journal Asiatique" VIIe série, Tome XX., No. 2, Août-Septembre 1882) dated in the Śaka year 589 "essentially agrees with those of the first Châḷukyas from the sixth to the eight century." The alphabet of the most ancient inscriptions found in Annam fully resembles, as has been remarked by M. Abel Bergaine (Journal Asiatique, Janvier 1888, page 15) the alphabets of the inscriptions of the kings of Vêṅgî, the Pallavas and the first Kadambas. Again, certain inscriptions (for example Nos 415 and 415 bis, XXI of the collection mentioned by Mr. Bergaine) are characterised by a peculiarity which is called the "box-headed" alphabet and M. Bergaine observes that "the relations between the Champà kingdom and those of Southern India were so frequent that the alphabet changed there in the same manner. We shall even see that a simple ornamental appendage, a deeply cut square at the head of the letters which, in India proper, seems to have been in fashion during almost the whole of the V century finds its way into our XXI inscription.

It must first be noted that this influence existed in the II century of the Christian era :

(1) The inscription of Mura-râja or Śrî Mara, king of the Champàs, which is found near the village of Vo-can, in the Nhatrang valley in the province of Khah-Hoo (Journal Asitique, Janv.-Fevrier. 1891, page 17) in Annam, is written in Sanskṛit and in an alphabet that is identical with that of the inscription of Rudradâman at Girnar.

(2) Ptolemy gives the names of the towns situated on the coast of Annam that were not simply Indian but were also Sanskṛit (Journal Asiatique-Rapport Annuel; Juillet-Août 1888, page 70).

We thus arrive at the following very important conclusion : "The Indo-Chinese civilisation did not come from every place in India, but, from a port of the Deccan whence the travellers embarked for Indo-China".

Where was this port situated ?. That is the important problem we are now going to solve. This port was existing at the time of Ptolemy, and is found mentioned by this geographer. In fact, this is how Ptolemy describes the east coast of the Deccan (see Ind. Ant., Vol. XIII., page 332) : "Mouth of the river

Khabêros—Khabêris—Sabouras—Podoukê—Melangê—Mouth of the river Tyna—Kottis—Manarpha—Mouth of the river Maisôlus—Kontakossyla, a mart—Koddura—Allosygnê—The point of departure for ships bound for Khrysê—Paloura—Naingaina—Katikardama— Kannagara—Mouth of the river Madana".

We see that, in the II century, Ptolemy has said that the ships that wanted to go to the country of gold (Khrysê) i. e. the Indo-Chinese peninsula (Burma, Malacca, Cambodia, Annam) started from a fixed point (locus unde solvunt in Chrysen navigantes). Till now there was complete uncertainty in regard to the geographical position of this port. There was no doubt at all that "Khabêris-emporium" designated the town of Kâv'rîpatnam; in fact, Ptolemy has mentioned above the "mouth of the river Khabêros" which is undoubtedly the Kâvêrî. But between this town and the Ganges not a single place mentioned by Ptolemy could be identified with some amount of certainty. Many authors have put forth hypotheses but without any great success. Colonel Yule thought that the river Maisôlus was no other than the Kṛishṇâ, because not far from its mouth there is the modern town of Masulipatam; but this reason was not very convincing. In the theory of Colonel Yule the town that Ptolemy calls Koddura was identified with Gûdûru, near Masulipatam. This identification was regarded with the greatest scepticism, for they replied to Colonel Yule that:

(1) The word Koddura does not fully resemble the word Gûdûru.

(2) There is nothing to prove that the village of Gûdûru existed at the time of Ptolemy and has preserved the same name for 18 centuries.

It is no more the same thing to-day. In compiling the ancient history of the Deccan and in studying the Koṇḍamudi plates, we have made the following important discoveries: (1) That the modern town named Gûdûru by Colonel Yule was once called Kudûra (2) that Kudûra existed at the time of Ptolemy. So we can now think of identifynig the Koddura of Ptolemy with the Kudûra of Koṇḍamudi plates.

Our knowledge of ancient Deccan enables us to make another new identification. Between Gûḍûru and the mouth of the

Kṛishṇâ, there is the town of Ghaṇṭaśàlà, where Mr. Alexandre Rea (South Indian Bouddhist Antiquities—Madras 1894, page 32) has discovered the remains of a Stûpa which date from the beginning of the Christian era ; so, Ghaṇṭaśâlâ existed at the time of Ptolemy ; and exactly at the required spot, on the sea side, between Koddura and the mouth of the river, Ptolemy places the mart of Kontakossyla.

We have thus solved an important problem, we have been able to identify certain places named by Ptolemy in a part of the Deccan coast ; and the place whence ships departed for Indo-China is found near Koddura, a little more to the north on the coast, i. e. not far from the mouth of the Godâvârî.

We shall therefore conclude that the port of departure for vessels bound for Khrysê, during the time of Ptolemy, was situated near the mouth of the Godâvârî and that it was from there that the civilisation of India starteed to go over to Burma, Java, Cambodia and Annam.

§ 3. The Śālaṅkāyanas.

This dynasty had Veṅgipura for its capital, and had a special cult for the god Chitrarathaswâmin. The remains of a temple dedicated to this deity are found at Pedda-vêgi near Ellore. As copper-plates connected with this dynasty and this country have been found in the environs of this town, I think we may admit the identity of Veṅgipura with Pedda-vêgi. The plates of king Vijaya-Dêvavarman (Ep. Ind. Vol. IX., No. 7, page 56) are in Prâkṛit but contain two sanskṛit verses. This king is said to be the 'performer of horse sacrifices.'

Another set of plates found near lake Kolleru (Ind. Ant. Vol. V., 1876, No. XVIII, page 175) is in Sanskṛit and is probably not so ancient. It mentions Chaṇḍavarman and his son Vijaya-Nandivarman. The Śâlaṅkâyanas ruled at this epoch over the same country of Kuḍuhâra which formerly was the native land of the Bṛihatphalâyanas.

And J. F. Fleet says (Ind. Ant. Vol. V., 1876, page 175): "In Sir W. Elliot's fac-similes I have another copper-plate inscription of Vijaya-Nandivarmâ and his Yuvamahârâja whose name seems to be Vijaya-Tuṅgavarma or Vijaya Buddhavarmâ .... the language, even, is doubtful but seems to be prâkṛit........." This name is probably Buddhavarmâ, for, in the margin there is the character "dha" ".

It is probable that these kings : Dêvavarman, Chaṇḍavarman, his son Nandivarman and perhaps also the problematical Buddhavarman, have reigned between 350 and 450 A. D. It appears in fact that these kings came after the invasion of Samudra-Gupta ; and it is again probable that their kingdom was conquered in the fifth century by the Vishṇukuṇḍins with the help of the Vâkâṭakas.

§ 4. The Vishṇukuṇḍins.

The Râmatîrtham (Ep. Ind. Vol. XI., page 134) and the Chikkulla plates (Ep. Ind. Vol. IV., page 193) give us genealogy No. I; and the Pulimbûru grant (Report on Epigraphy for 1913-14; G. O. No. 920, Public, 4th Aug. 1914, page 102) gives us genealogy No. II:

No I.
- Mâdhavavarman I.
- Vikramêndravarman I.
- Indrabhaṭṭârakavarman
- Vikramêndravarman II.

No II.
- Vikramahêndra
- Govindavarman
- Mâdhavavarman (II).

I am of opinion that Vikramahêndra may be identified with Vikramêndravarman II. In fact, I have remarked that in several documents the information regarding the grand-father or other ancestors of the reigning king has been sometimes altered. It is probable that the real name of the grandfather of Mâdhava II was Vikramêndravarman II.

It seems that the capital of the kingdom was Lenduḷûra which is probably the present village of Dendulûru, in the Ellore taluq near the ancient city of Veṅgî.

The tutelary deity of the dynasty is the "Holy Lord of Śrî Parvata," Śrî Sailam in the Karnul District. This God was the favourite deity of Prabhâvatî, widow of Rudrasêna II. and mother of Pravarasêna II, the Vâkâṭaka king. On the other hand, Mâdhavavarman I., the first Vishṇukuṇḍin king had married a Vâkâṭaka princess and we have said already, that very probably, in the middle of the V century, the Vâkâṭakas uprooted the ancient Śâlaṅkâyana dynasty of Vengî and placed on the throne their relation Mâdhavavarman I. This king, in fact, is reported to have performed numerous sacrifices, 11 of them being horse sacrifices which are emblems of victory. Besides that, the eulogies of this king resemble those found in the Vâkâṭaka copper-plates of Pravarasêna I.

The king Vikramêndravarman I. had no other merit than that of birth. He was the ornament of two families, the Vishṇukuṇḍins and the Vâkâṭakas. His reign was probably short.

On the contrary, Indrabhaṭṭârakavarman had a long reign as the Râmatirtham plates are dated in the 37th year of his reign; besides, during this reign, there was a terrible attack made by a king, who probably reigned in Kaliṅga, who was also called "Indra" and who seems to have been the head of a coalition of kings. These plates tell us that Indrabhaṭṭârakavarman "encountered in hundred thousands of battles numerous four-tusked elephants (chaturdanta)"; we know that God Indra is mounted on the elephant of the East which has four tusks. That statement is wholly confirmed by copper plates written in a similar alphabet which have been found in the Gôdaveri District. They are those of Pṛithivimûla (J. B. B. R. A. S., Vol. XVI., page 116). From lines 17-20, we learn an alliance was entered into by several chiefs to uproot by force Indrabhaṭṭâraka whose élephant Kumuda (the elephant of the S. W. quarter) was struck down by Indrâdhirâja mounted on his own elephant Supratika (the elephant of N. E. quarter). So there were two Indras present: Indrâdhirâja, king of the northeast, that is, of Kaliṅga along the coast of Orissa, and Indrabhaṭṭâraka, the Vishṇukuṇḍin who reigned in the southwest, that is to say in Vêṅgi. Now, it seems that it was the king of the Vishṇukuṇḍins that was the victor. In fact the same Râmatirtham plates commemorate the grant made by Indra of a village situated in the Plaki-rashtra. This province is mentioned in the Timmapuram plates (Ep. Ind. Vol. IX., page 317) under the name of Paḷaki-vishaya. And we know that this same province of Paḷaki-vishaya contained the village of Cheṛûpûra, which is nothing but Chipurupalli in the Vizagapatam District (Ind. Ant. Vol. XX., pages 15 and 16). Since the Vishṇukuṇḍin Indra was the master of Vizagapatam District after his war with the king of Orissa, it is certain that he was the victor. We have said that there was a coalition of many kings against Indrabhaṭṭâraka. Among them perhaps was Harishêna the Vâkâṭaka;

in fact, the Ajaṇṭâ inscription says that Harishêna vanquished the king of the Ândhra country. This word shows the country between the Gôdâvari and the Kṛishṇâ, that is to say, the kingdom of the Vishṇukuṇdins.

The son of Indrabhaṭṭâraka was Vikramêndravarman II. It is certain that this king reigned on the banks of the Kṛishṇâ as the Chikkulla plates mention the village of Régonṛam to the S. E. of Râvirêva on the bank of the Kṛishṇabennâ ; and Râvirêva has been identified by Mr. Sewell with Raveralah 80°10'E and 16°50'N) :

The son of Vikramêndravarman II. (Vikramahêndra) was Gôvindavarman and his grandson Mâdhavavarman II (Janâśrâya). The last of them "crossed the river Gôdâvarî with the desire to conquer the eastern region". This event probably took place shortly before the invasion of Pulakêśin II. who put an end to the dynasty of Vishṇukuṇḍins and annexed the kingdom of Vêngî.

In my work "The Pallavas" (chapter III., page 34), I have attributed the caves of Unḍavalli, Sittanagaram, Bezwâda, Mogalrâjapuram to the Vishṇukuṇdins. I shall not speak of it once again.

The seal of the Chikkula plates (Ep. Ind. Vol IV., plate facing the page 244) resembles that of the Râmatîrtham plates: an advancing lion with its fore-paw raised, mouth wide open and the tail swung over the back so as to end in a loop (G. O. No. 538 ; Rep. on Epi. 28th July 1909). The lion was then the crest of the Vishṇukuṇḍins. It is to be remarked that the Kadambas have the same crest which proves the family relationship that existed between the Kadambas and the Vishṇukuṇḍins. We find the image of a vase sculptured on the pillars at Uṇḍavalli and Mogalrâzapuram, and the image of a lion at Uṇḍavalli. Coins bearing the image of a lion on the obverse and the image of a vase on the reverse have also been found. (see for instance, in Mr. Vincent A. Smith's, "Early History of India," the plate concerning the Indian coins in the British Museum : coin No. 16, from Elliot, "Coins of Southern India" Pl., II, 49). These coins have been attributed to the Pallavas. In 1917, in my work "The Pallavas" (Chapter III, page 34), I have attributed these coins to the Vishṇukuṇḍins.

§ 5. The Kings of Kaliṅga.

We have six documents that give us information about the kings of Kaliṅga. We have said that, about A. D. 340, Samudra-Gupta met on the coast of Orissa with Maṇṭarâja, king of Korâla, Swâmidatta of Koṭṭûra, Damana of Eraṇḍapali and Mahêndra of Pishṭâpura. The last of them had probably the title of king of Kaliṅga : we shall see, in fact, that Śaktivarman (Ragolu plates) who also reigned at Pishṭapura had this title. The six documents we have mentioned being all in Sanskṛit are probably posterior to the year 400 A. D. On the other hand the coast of Orissa was conquered by Pulakêśin II (Aihole inscription) about 609 A. D. and was probably shared between the Eastern Châḷukyas in the south and the Eastern Gaṅgas in the north. The dates of the 6 documents in question are therefore between 400 and 600 A. D.

Unfortunately, it is impossible to establish a chronology of the kings of Kaliṅga whose names we know. Therefore we shall now proceed to enumerate those documents without any ascertained chronological order.

a) The Ragolu plates (Ep. Ind. Vol XII, page 2) mention Vâsishṭhiputra Śaktivarman, king of Kaliṅga who reigned at Pishṭâpura. It is said that this sovereign "adorns the Mâgadha family," which goes to show that this prince was related to the Guptas and reigned towards the middle of the V century when the Guptas and the Vâkâṭakas dominated the Deccan.

b) The Gôdâvari copper plates (J. B. B. R. A. S. Vol XVI, page 116) had been studied when we gave the history of Indrabhaṭṭâraka of the Vishṇukuṇḍin dynasty : the king Pṛithivimula who was the donor of the Gôdâvari plates was the son of Śrî-Prabhâkara and reigned in the city of Kâṇḍâḷi. He was the vassal of another more powerful king named Indra who was the son of Mitavarman, reigned at Maṇalkudi and had for his war-elephent Supratika (the elephent of the N. E. quarter). The document says that this king was the victor in the struggle against the king Indrabhaṭṭâraka. But we have said that this is not probable and that, on the contrary, the Vishṇukuṇḍin king seems to have aennxed the districts of Gôdâvari and Vizagapatam and driven away the kings of Kaliṅga to the north. In fact, the capital of the kings of Kaliṅga which was Pishṭâpuram at the times of Mahêndra and Vâsisṭhiputra Śaktivarman seems to have been transferred further north to Sârapalli and Siṁhapura after the Vishṇukuṇḍins captured Pishṭâpuram. This event probably took place in the first quarter of the VI Century.

c) The Chikakole plates (Ind. Ant. Vol. XIII., page 48) of Nandaprabhañjanavarman issued from Sârapalli and

d) the Kômarti plates (Ep. Ind. Vol. IV., page 143) of Chandavarman issued from Siṁhapuram, have many points of resemblance: the phraseology of both these documents is almost the same; the seals bear the word "Pitṛibhaktah"; Nandaprabhañjana and Chandavarman are both of them called kings of Kaliṅga; and lastly, Siṁhapura, the capital of Chandavarman may be identified with Siṅgupuram, a village neâr Chikakole where the plates of Nandaprabhañjana were discovered.

e) The Brihaṭprôsṭha grant of Umâvarman, lord of Kaliṅga, issued from Siṁhapura (Ep. Ind., Vol. XII., page 4) surely belongs to the same group as the plates of Chikakole and Kômarti. It is impossible to say in what chronological order, Umâvarman, Nandaprabhañjana and Chandravarman reigned. Their epoch is also uncertain; they might possibly have reigned between 525 and 609 A. D.

f) Lastly, we have to mention the Sarabhavaram plates (Ep. Ind., Vol. XIII., page 104) for, this village where they were discovered is in the Gôdâvarî district and it is probably here that the Lord of Chikûra, whose name is not mentioned and who perhaps lived in the VI century, reigned. He was probably not a "king of Kaliṅga" but only a simple feudatory.

CHAPTER VII.

THE DYNASTIES OF THE KANARESE DISTRICTS.

§ 1. The Kadambas.

The genealogy of the Kadambas may probably be the following:

- Mayûraśarman (340-360 A. D.)
  - Kaṅgavarman (360-385 A. D.)
    - Bhagîratha (385-410 A. D.)
      - Raghu (410-425 A. D.)
      - Kâkusthavarman (425-450 A. D.)
        - Santivarman (450-475 A. D.)
          - Mṛigêśavarman (475-488 A. D.)
            - Ravivarman (500-537 A. D.)
              - Harivarman (537-550 A. D.)
            - Bhânuvarman
            - Śivaratha
          - Mândhâtṛivarman (488-500 A. D.)
        - Kṛishṇavarman I.
          - Vishṇuvarman
            - Siṁhavarman
              - Kṛishṇavarman II. (550-565 A. D.)
                - Ajavarman
                  - Bhogivarman
                    - Vishṇuvarman etc.
          - Dêvavarman

- Kumaravarman
  - Mandhata-Râja (Shimoga plates)

A part of this genealogy has been published by Professor Kielhorn (Ep. Ind., Vol. VIII., page 30) and admitted by Mr. Rice in his work "Mysore and Coorg from inscriptions" ["jyêshṭha-pitṛi," in the Bîrûr plates, means a father's elder brother].

The genealogy given above differs from those published by Messrs. Kielhorn and Rice because I have taken into account the discovery of the Shimoga plates in 1911 and those of Tagare in 1918. The Tagare plates (Annual Report, Mysore Archæological Department, for 1918, page 40, No. 71) give us the following genealogy:

Kṛishṇavarman
|
Ajavarman
|
Bhôgivarman
|
Vishṇuvarman

Relying on the form of the letters, I thought that it was not possible to admit that this Kṛishṇavarman was Kṛishnavarman I ; but that he was, on the contrary, very probably Kṛishṇavarman II.

The Shimoga plates (Annual Report, Mysore Archæological Department, for 1911, page 31), say that the king Mândhâta-Râja, son of Kumâravarman reigned at Uchchangi (Uchchangidurga=Uchchaśriṅgi). This town belonged to Śivaratha in the 4th year of the reign of Harivarman (Halsî plates, Ind. Ant., Vol., page 30); that is why we can suppose that Kumâravarman was the son of Śivaratha or Harivarman; the Shimoga plates do not give us any information about his filiation.

The chronology of the Kadambas has not yet been fixed on a sure basis. It is only a complete study not only of this dynasty but also of all the other dynasties of the Deccan that will enable us to arrive at a satisfactory result. In the genealogical table, I have just given, I have put within brackets, beside the name of each king, the approximate date of his reign, according to the chronology I have adopted. I shall now try to justify this chronology.

(1) We have said, when speaking of the copper plates of the Pallava dynasty, that palæography was generally a bad auxiliary to the chronology of dynasties; very often, two documents dated in the same reign differ much from each other. However there is a special case to which I must draw the reader's attention. We know that in the middle of the V century the Gupta-Vâkâṭakas were very powerful in the Deccan. I call Gupta-Vâkâṭakas those kings of the Vâkâṭaka dynasty who were the sons, grandsons or great-grandsons of queen Prabhâvati, daughter of Dêvagupta (Chandra-Gupta II). We know that this queen was the regent of the kingdom during the miniority of her son; and the plates of Professor Pâtak (Ind. Ant., 1912, page 215), which are dated in the time of this princess, bear on the seal not the genealogy of the Vâkâṭakas but of the Guptas. The descendants of this queen considered themselves to be as much Guptas as Vâkâṭakas. They adopted a very peculiar alphabet which spread as a queer fashion in the V century, in the empire of the Guptas, at the time of Chandra-Gupta II (Bühler "Ind. paleography" Ind. Ant. Vol XXXIII, page 64). This has been styled the "box-headed" alphabet. I distinguish two sorts of "box" placed at the head of the letters :

The "true box" ; it is thus described by J. F. Fleet : "formed by sinking four short strokes in the shape of a square and leaving a block of stone or copper in the centre of them" (Gupta Inscriptions, page 19).

The "false box" is more simple: the sculptor or engraver has simply removed a sufficiently large square surface at the head of each letter.

As an example of the "true box" we may take the Balaghat plates (Ep. Ind. Vol. IX., page 268) of Prithivishêṇa II and all the plates of Pravarasêna II (Chammak, Siwani and Dudia).

When examining the Uruvupalli plates (see the plate in Ind. Ant. Vol. V, page 51) which are dated from Palakkada in the 11th year of the reign of the Pallava king Simhavarman and which have been engraved by order of Yuvamahârâja Vishṇugôpa, I made the important remark, which no one has done up to the present, that the alphabet of this documents was "box headed" ; nay more, it is not the "false box" but the "true box" so much so that these plates can be shown as an excellent specimen of the "true box". Siṁhavarman and Vishṇugôpa have reigned between 475 and 500 A. D. and the Uruvupalli plates are probably dated 486 A. D. The plates of Mâṅgaḷûr and Pikira of the son of Vishṇugôpa are not box-headed; we may therefore say that from 500 A. D., the box method disappeared. The same phenomenon is to be seen in the Kadamba documents: the plates of Mṛigêśa and Mândhaṭri are box-headed, but those of Ravivarman are not. There is room to think that Mṛigêsa and Mândhâṭri reigned from 475 to 500 A. D. and were contemporaries of Siṁhavarman and Vishṇugôpa; and that Ravivarman reigned after 500 A. D. when the box method has disappeared from the Deccan.

(2) We know that about 550 A. D., Pulakêśin I seized Vâtâpî and founded the Chaḷukya kingdom: but if we look at the map, we see that the geographical position of Bâdâmî (Vâtâpî) allows us to affirm that Palâśikâ (Halsi) could not belong to the Kadambas when the Châḷukyas were in Bâdâmî. It may therefore be asserted that all the plates found at Halsi and dated from Palâśikâ (Ind. Ant., Vol. VI, pages 23, 25, 28, 29, 31,) are anterior to 550 A. D. We may therefore say that Harivarman who, in the 5th year of his reign (Ind. Ant., Vol. VI, page 31) held Palâśikâ, reigned there before the middle of the VI century. It has to be noted that we do not know of any Kadamba document dated from Palâśikâ which is posterior to the one we have just mentioned; it is therefore probable that Harivarman was almost the contemporary of Puḷakêśin I and was vanquished by him. The Sangoli plates (Ep. Ind., Vol. XIV, page 165) mention an astronomical phenomenon and Mr. K. N. Dikshit of Poona has observed that during the VI century this phenomenon could have occured only thrice: in 507, in 526 and in 545. The Sangoli plates being dated in the 8th year of Harivarman's reign, this king must have come to the throne only in 526-8=518 A. D. or in 545-8=537 A. D., if we believe that this event happened in the VI century. The latter date agrees perfectly well with the chronology we have adopted; we shall therefore admit that Harivarman ascended the throne in 537 A. D.

Let us now proceed to sum up the history of this dynasty.

The Tâḷaguṇḍa inscription (Ep. Ind., Vol VIII, page 30) gives a version, probably historical, of the origin of the Kadambas. There was a brahman belonging to the Mânavya gôtra named Mayûraśarman who was a native of Sthânakundur (Tâḷguṇḍa) and belonged to a family called Kadamba since a kadamba tree sheltered their house. He came to the capital of the Pallava empire to study the Vèdas and there had a quarrel with a horseman. Hearing it said that the brahman caste was inferior to that of the Kshatrias, he got angry, put himself at the head of a band of adventurers and attacked the Pallavas in the forests of Srî Parvata. With the help of Bṛihad-Bâna and other kings, he succeeded in founding the kingdom of which Banavâsi (Vaijayanti) was the capital. Mr. K. G. Sankara Iyer of Trivandram in his excellent article on "The age of Kâlidâsa" published in the "Quarterly Journal of the Mythic Society," (Bangalore, Vol. VIII., July 1918) says: "It is probable that Mâyuraśarman took advantage of the confusion caused by Samudragupta's southern expedition to set himself up as an independent ruler". This hypothesis accords with the chronology we have adopted.

Dr. A. Venkatasubbiah, the learned officer of the "Mysore Archæological Department", has written an article on "The Kadamba prâkṛit inscription of Malavalli" Ind, Ant., Vol. XLVI, page 154), in which we find the exact tenor of that document. It is a Kadamba inscription, but the name of the king is not mentioned. However, as it is in prâkṛit we may suppose that he was the most ancient king of the dynasty and that the document is dated in the reign of Mayuraśarman, that is, the middle of the IV century.

The 8th verse of the Ajaṇṭâ inscription (cave No. XVI, Arch. Surv. W. Ind., Vol IV, pages 53 and 124) says that the Vâkâṭaka king Prithivishêṇa I. vanquished the king of Kuntala, i. e. the Kadamba king. It is certain that Prithivishêṇa I. reigned for a long time: tradition says that he reigned for about a hundred years and Mr. Vincent A. Smith is of opinion that it means "from about forty to sixty years". We know that his son Rudrasêna II. married the daughter of Chandra-Gupta II. about 395 A. D. We may therefore be almost sure that Pṛithivishêṇa I. reigned between 350 and 390 A. D. According to our chronology he must have been the contemporary of the Kadamba king Kaṅgavarman (360-385 A. D.) and it is probable that this king of Kuntala is the one whose defeat is mentioned in the Ajaṇṭâ inscription; and the Tâḷguṇḍa inscription seems to confirm this supposition, as it says that Kaṅgavarman accomplished "lofty exploits in terrible wars".

We have not got any information about Bhagîratha.

Raghu "subdued enemies by his valour". It is probably in his reign that his brother Kâkustha bore the title of Yuvamahârâja and ruled over Palâśikâ (Halsi in Belgaum) in the year 80 of an unknown era which probably began with the founding of the dynasty by Mayûraśarman. In that case, the Halsi plates (Ind. Ant., Vol. VI, page 23) would be dated about the year 420 A. D. and Kâkustha would have come to the throne in 425 and reigned till 450 A. D.

The Balaghat plates (Ep. Ind., Vol. IX., page 268) say that Narêndrasêna was the grandson of Prabhâvati-Guptâ and that he married the daughter of the king of Kuntala named Ajjhitabhaṭṭarikâ. When did this marriage take place? We have admitted with Mr. Vincent A. Smith (J. R. A. S., April 1914, page 326) that the marriage of Rudrasâna II with the daughter of Chandra-Gupta II, the queen Prabhâvati-Gupta, took place about 395 A. D.; we may suppose that the marriage of their grandson took place 50 years later. So the marriage of the prince Gupta-Vâkâṭaka with the daughter of the king of Kuntaḷa must be placed about 445 A. D. We have said above that it is certain that the Kunṭala kingdom was no other than the kingdom of the Kadambas (see Ep. Ind., Vol. XIII, page 299, verses 58—62). We may therefore put the question: who was the Kadamba king that reigned in 445 and gave his daugter in marriage to the Gupta-Vâkâṭaka king? In our chronology Kâkusthavarman is shown to have reigned from 425 to 450 and it is quite possible that in 445 he had a daughter of marriageable age: and the celebrated inscription of Tâḷaguṇḍa which contains the eulogy of Kâkusthavarman and is writhen in the "box-headed" alphabet says that Kâkusthavarman gave his daughters in marriage to the Guptas and other kings.

The plates of Mṛigêśa and Mândhâtṛi, "the sons of Śântivarman, are also written in the same alphabet.

Two sets of copper plates discovered at Dêvagiri (Ind. Ant., Vol. VII, page 35 and page 37) are dated in the 3rd and 4th years of the reign of Mṛigêśa; the Halsi plates (Ind. Ant., Vol. VI, p, 24) and the Hire-Sakuna plates (Ep. Carn,, VIII, page 12), are dated in the 8th year of the same reign. The Hiṭṇahabbâgilu (Ep. Carn., IV, p. 136) and Tâḷguṇḍa records are not dated. The last document (Mysore Archæological Report. for 1910-11, page 35, and Plate IV, 2) mentions the wife of Mṛigêśa, who was born in the Kaikeya family, and was called Prâbhâvati. In the first 8 years of his reign, about 480 A. D. Mṛigêśa utprooted the Gaṅgas, and was a very fire of destruction of the Pallavas (Halsi plates, Ind. Ant., VI, p. 24). Mṛigêśa reigned at Vaijayanti. It is probable that he did not reign long, since the documents we have got do not go beyond the 8th year of his reign.

It is probable that Mṛigêśa was succeeded by his younger brother Mândhâṭrivarman who also reigned at Vaijayanti: the Kûḍgere plates (Ep. Ind., Vol. VI., p. 14) are dated in the 2nd year of his reign. His private secretary Dâmôdaradatta was probably the Dâmôdara of Koṇṇûr (Ind. Ant., Vol. XXI., p. 93).

In the absence of more precise information, we may admit that Mṛigêśa reigned from 475 to 490 A. D. and Mândhâṭri from 490 to 500 A. D.

When Śantivarman, Mṛigêśa and Mândhaṭri were reigning at Vaijayanti, the northern provinces (Belgaum, Kaladgee and Darwar), which had Palâśikâ (Halsi) and Triparvata (probably Dêvagêri) for their capitals, were governed by princes belonging to the younger branch of the Kadamba family. Kṛishṇavarman I., son of Kâkustha and elder brother of Santivarman, reigned at Triparvata (probably Dêvagêri, in the Karajgi taluk of Dhârwâḍ District). He had the prince Dêvavarman as yuvamahârâja (Dêvagêre plates, Ind. Ant., Vol. VIII., p. 33). Almost at the same time, Vishṇuvarman, the elder (Birur plates) son of Kṛishṇavarman I, made a grant in the Sindhuthaya-rashtra (Bijapur District) with the permission of his consin Santivarman (Birur plates; Ep. Carn., Vol. VI., p. 91; Kadur No. 162) Vishṇuvarman was the son of a Kaikêya princess who had married Krishnavarman I. Who were the Kaikeyas? Nothing is known about them. The kingdom of Palâśikâ (Halsi), which was governed by Vishṇuvarman, belonged to the Kadambas of Vaijayanti.; in fact, when Mṛigêśa was reigning at Vaijayantî (Ind. Ant., vol. VI, page 24), he gave orders for the construction of a temple at Palâśikâ.

It is probable that on the death of Mândhaṭri, the crown of the Kadambas came, as a matter of right, to Ravivarman the son of Mândhaṭri; this prince being young, his cousin Vishṇuvarman tried to size upon the throne with the help of the Pallavas; but Ravi killed his adversary. In fact, a set of Halsi plates (Ind. Ant., Vol. VI, page 32) say that Râvivarman "acquired the regal power by the strength and prowess of his own arm", and another set of Halsi plates (Ind. Ant., Vol. VI, page 29) also add that Râvivarman "having slain Śrî-Vishṇuvarman and other kings, and having uprooted Chaṇḍadanda, the lord of Kâñchi has established himself at Palâśikâ". The Nilambur plates (Ep. Ind., Vol. VIII., page 146) are dated in the 5th year of Ravivarman's reign; and there are three sets of plates (Ind. Ant., Vol. VI, page 25, 28 and 29) that are dated in the same reign from Palâśikâ. The Ajjibad-Sirsi plates (Progress Report, Arch. Surv. West. Ind., for 1917-1918, page 35) are dated in the 35th year of his reign which corresponds probably to circ. 535 A. D. and it is likely, that, having come to the throne about 500 A. D. when sufficiently young, he reigned for about 40 years and died in 537 A. D. The inscription on the stone at Kavaḍi (Sorab 523, Shimoga; (Ep. Carn., Vol. VIII, page 167) mentions the death of Ravi and of his wife who probably became a sati.

His son Harivarman succeeded him at Vaijayantî (Sangoli plates; Ep. Ind., Vol. XIV., page 165; 8th year of the reign) and at Palâśikâ (Halsi plates, Ind. Ant., Vol. VI., page 31; 5th year of his reign). We have said that he ascended the throne in 537 A. D.

About the year 550 A. D., Pulakêśin I. of the Chaḷukya family installed himself at Vâtâpi (Bâdâmi). This town being situated exactly in the middle of the northern provinces of the Kadamba kingdom, it is almost certain that Harivarman lost, about 550 A. D., all the country that had for its capitals Palâśikâ (Haḷsi) and Triparvata.

We have seen that Ravivarman killed Vishṇuvarman, his cousin and settled at Palâśikâ; Siṁhavarman, the son of Visṇuvarman, probably remained in an inferior position during the reign of Ravivarman; but the son of Siṁhâvarman who was called Kṛishṇavarman II. ascended the throne of Vaijayanti. The Beṇṇur plates (Ep. Carn., Vol. V., page 594 ; Belur 245) speak of a military expedition and the Bennahalli plates (Ep. Carn., Vol. V, Be. 121 ; and Ep. Ind., Vol. VI., page 18) say that Kṛishṇavarman II. "has gained the fortune of royalty by his heroism". The kingdom of Kṛishṇavarman II. extended between the Chaḷukya kingdom in the north and that of the Gaṅgas in the south. Mâdhava II. of the Gaṅga dynasty married the sister of Kṛishṇavarman II. Probably, it was Kṛishṇavarman II. that was defeated by the Chaḷuka Kîrtivarman I. shortly before 570 A. D. and whose country was ruined by the Pallavas (Aṇaji insc., Ep. Carn., Vol. XI, Dg, No. 161).

For a long time it was believed that the dynasty was completely destroyed. However, the discovery of the Tagare plates (Mysore Arch. Report for 1918, page 40 and plate XI) seems to prove that the son of Kṛishṇavarman II. who was called Ajavarman, did not reign, but that Bhôgivarman, the son of Ajavarman, was the "acquirer of an extensive kingdom by the strength of his own arm". It is probable that this kingdom did not last long, for, it appears that this country was occupied, shortly after, by the Gaṅgas (Tagare plates of Polavîra, Mysore Arch. Report for 1918, page 41). Vishṇuvarman son of Bhôgivarman probably lived in the beginning of the VII century.

The Châḷukya king Puḷakeśin II besieged Banavâsî (Aihole insc.) and, in the Kadamba country there are inscriptions of Puḷakêśin II (Sh, 10), Vikramâditya (Sa. 79), Vinayâditya (Sn. 154) and Vijayâditya (Sk. 278).

At the end of the VIII century, the Pallava king Dantivarman married Aggaḷanimmaṭi, "the daughter of the celebrated king, a crest jewel of the Kadamba family" (Vêlûrpâḷaiyam plates, vers 18 ; S. I. I., Vol. II., Part V., page 511).

§ 2. The Gaṅgas.

Up to the moment of writing this, the genealogy of this dynasty has remained unsettled for the following reasons: The first documents that were discovered were no doubt spurious. They gave the following genealogy:

Koṅgaṇivarman,
|
Mâdhava (I),
|
Harivarman,
|
Kishṇugôpa,
|
Mâdhava (II),
|
Avinîta,
etc.

In 1913, were discovered the Penukoṇḍa plates which give the following genealogy:

Koṅgaṇivarman,
|
Mâdhava,
|
Âyyavarman,
|
Madhava.

This document was certainly a genuine one; it was admitted that the genealogy given in the spurious records is erroneous and that the only reliable one is what is given in the Penukoṇḍa plates. It has therefore been admitted that the following is the correct genealogy:

Koṅgaṇivarman,
|
Mâdhava
|
Âyyavarman,
|
Mâdhava II.,
|
Avinîta,
etc.

Here the donor of the Penukoṇḍa plates is mentioned as the father of Avinita. I strongly protest against these suppositions. I affirm that the genealogy given in the spurious records is quite correct, but that, till now, no one has understood the true reason for the disagreement that exists between the Penukoṇḍa plates and the other documents. F. Fleet says (J. R. A. S., 1915, page 472): "It must be obvious that two such different statements cannot both be true". There lies the mistake: I am of opinion that both the genealogies are correct; but they are of two different dynasties.

First of all, I have to declare most emphatically that the genealogy given in the spurious records is quite correct. In the Mysore Archæological Report for 1916, Mr. R. Narasimhachar has published two sets of copper plates: the Sringeri plates of Avinîta and the Uttanur plates of Durvinîta; and, as for the Gummareḍḍipura plates of the same king published in 1912 § 69, "there are no indications, that would lead one to suspect the genuineness" of those records. The dynasty referred to in these documents is that of the "Gaṅgas of Talakâḍ".

I now proceed to prove the existence of a second dynasty which I shall call the dynasty of the "Gaṅgas of Paruvi". We possess two documents of this dynasty which has remained unknown till now:

1) The Penukoṇḍa plates issued by the king Mâdhava when making a grant of land situated near the tank of Paruvi in Paravivishaya (J. R. A. S., 1915, page 480 and "Report on Epigraphy" for 1913-1914, Madras, page 83-84);

2) The Benḍigânhalli plates of Kṛishṇavarman, son of Mâdhava, which mentions the grant of Kuraura in Paruvishaya (Mysore Archæol. Annual Report for 1914-1915, plate XVIII). Paruvi is identical with Parigi seven miles north of Hindupur in the Anantapur district.

The capital of this dynasty was perhaps Kavaipâṭa from which place are dated the plates of Kṛishṇavarman.

The chronology of the Gaṅgas has till now remained so very uncertain that the authors who have treated the subject sometimes differ by several centuries.

However, all of them are almost agreed on the one point, that Mâdhava II, the father of Avinîta, married the sister of Kṛishṇavarman I, the son of Kâkusthavarman of the Kadamba dynasty : but it is quite certain it was not the case. The documents say that Mâdhava II. married the sister of the Kadamba Kṛishṇavarman, but this king was, I am sure, the second of that name and not the first. I declare that Mâdhava II. married the sister of Kṛishṇavarman II.

The first king, of whose date we are sure, reigned in the VIII century : in 1918, Mr. R. Narasimhachar discovered at Halkûr (Sîra taluk) an inscription on a stone belonging to the reign of Śrîpurusha and dated Ś. 710 or 788 A. D. This king was the son of Śivamâra (Vaḷḷimalai insc., No. 91 of 1889), and grandson (Śûḍi plates, Ep. Ind., Vol. VIII, p. 181), of Bhûvikrama. Since Śripurusha reigned in 788 A. D. we may suppose that his grand father Bhûvikrama ascended the throne in the first quarter of the VIII century (700-725 A. D.). The father of Bhûvikrama named Śrîvikrama must have reigned therefore in the 4th quarter of the VII century (675-700 A. D.) and his grandfather Mushkara in the 3rd quarter of the same century (650-675 A. D.). We know that Durvinîta the father of Mushkara reigned for a long time : the Gummareḍḍipura plates (Report, Archæol. Depart. Mysore, for 1912; paras 65-69) are, in fact, dated in the 40th year of his reign, and, as it is probable that he lived a few years more, we may give him a reign of 45 years which will extend from 605 to 650 A. D. His father Avinita probably reigned for an equally long period, for, the Śringêri plates, which are dated in the second year of his reign, say that he obtained the "sovereignty while still on the lap of his divine mother" and the grant of Ep. Carn., 9, Doḍḍa-Baḷḷâpûr, 68, is dated in the 29th year of his reign. We may therefore believe that he reigned for a further period of 11 years after making the latter grant and that his reign lasted about 40 years. Avinîta would therefore have reigned from 565 to 605 A. D. According to these calculations, Mâdhava II., the father of Avinîta, would have reigned from 540 to 565 A. D. and this is exactly the epoch we have assigned to the Kadamba Kṛishṇavarman II. If we now bear in mind that the Gaṅga Màdhava II. and the Kadamba Kṛishṇavarman II. both reigned over Mysore, the one in the North and the other in the South, and that, in consequence, they were neighbours, it would seem to be quite natural that Mâdhava II. should marry the sister of Kṛishṇavarman II. It is clear that it is absolutely impossible that Mâdhava II, who lived in the middle of the VI century, should have married the sister of Kṛishṇavarman I. who lived in the middle of the V century. We shall therefore conclude by saying : "Mâdhava II, the father of Avinîta, married the sister of the Kadamba Kṛishṇavarman II. and reigned from 540 to 565 A. D.".

This chronology is in perfect accord with all the documents. We shall presently see that Âyyavarman was placed on the throne about 480 A. D., by Siṁhavarman, the Pallava king that reigned from 475 to 500 A. D., and that the son of Âyyavarman was crowned by the Pallava Skandavarman (500-525 A. D.).

We get therefore the following genealogy and chronology :

Koṅganivarman, (of the Kaṇvâyana gôtra),
|
Mâdhava I.,
|

Âyyavarman (480-505)	Harivarman
|	|
Mâdhava (505-530)	Vishṇugôpa
|	|
Kṛishṇavarman (acc. circ. 530) (Paruvi dynasty)	Mâdhava II (540-565)
	|
	Avinita (565-605)
	|
	Durvinita (605-650)
	|
	Mushkara, | Śrîvikrama } second half of the VII century
	|
	Bhûvikrama, | Śivamâra } first half of the VIII century
	|
	Śrîpurusha (788 A. D.)
	etc.

We shall now try to give the history of these kings.

We have said that, about 480 A. D., the Kadamba Mṛigeśa fought with the Gaṅgas and was "a very fire of destruction of the Pallavas" (Halsi plates, Ind. Ant., Vol. VI., page 25). This information is very important as it proves that about 480 A. D. the Pallavas aided the Gaṅgas in their fight with the Kadambas. The Pallava king at this epoch was probably Siṁhavarman who reigned at Kâñchî and to whom we have assigned the date 475 to 500 A. D.; and this fact is confirmed by the Penugoṇḍa plates that say that the Gaṅga king Âyyavarman "was duly installed on the throne by Siṁhavarman Mahârâja, the lord of the prosperous Pallava family (Rep. on Ep. for 1913-14; G. O., No. 920, 4th Aug. 1914). The son of Âyyavarman who was called Mâdhava alias Siṁhavarman was "installed on the throne by the illustrious Pallava (king) Skandavarman". We have said that Skandavarman of Kâñchi, son of Siṁhavarman reigned from 500 to 525 A. D. It is probable that this Pallava king had also to contend with the Kadambas for strengthening the sovereignty of the Gaṅga king for, the Halsi plates (Ind. Ant., Vol. VI., p. 29) say that Râvivarman struggled against "Chaṇḍadanda, the lord of Kâñchî". Since we do not know of any Pallava king of that name, we may suppose that the name "Chandanda" was a "biruda" of Skandavarman who reigned at this epoch (500-525 A. D.)

Mâdhava alias Siṁhavarman, who made the grant commemorated by the Penugoṇḍa plates, reigned over Paruvishaya and must be identified with the Madhâva of the Benḍigânhalli plates (Mysore Archæ. Report for 1914-15, plate XIII) whose son Vijaya-Kṛishṇavarman reigned over Paruvishaya. This king Kṛishṇavarman must have reigned in the middle of the VI century, for, the alphabet of the Benḍigânhalli plates is almost identical with that of the Bannahalli (Ep. Ind, Vol. VI, p. 18) and Chikkulla (Ep. Ind., Vol. IV., p. 196) plates. Kṛishṇavarman is the last known king of the Paruvi dynasty.

The king Mâdhava II, who belonged to the dynasty of the Gaṅgas of Talakâḍ, "bought the sovereignty with the strength of his own arm", and married the younger sister of the Kadamba Kṛishṇavarman (II), who, in the middle of the VI century, reigned over a large part of Mysore.

His son Avinîta (565-605 A. D.) married the daughter of Skandavarman king of Punnâṭa.

We must here say a few words about the kings of Punnâḍ. The capital of this province was Kitthipura or Kittûr (Hg. 56, Ep. Carn., Vol. IV) on the river Kabbani, to the west of Talakâḍ. In 1917, Mr. R. Narasiṁhachar discovered (Mysore Archæol. Report for 1917, page 40, No. 87) the Mâmballi plates that give us reliable information about this dynasty. The spurious plates of Kômaraliṅgam (Ind. Ant., Vol. XVIII; page 362) give further details which are very probably historical.

The genealogy of this dynasty would be the following :

Râshṭravarman
(of the Tâmra-Kâśyapa family)

- Prithivipati (the eldest)
- Nâgadatta
  - Bhujaṅga (who married the daughter of Singavarman)
    - Skandavarman.

It is probable that this Skandavarman gave his daughter in marriage to the Gaṅga Avinîta (565-605 A. D.), king of Talakâḍ. The issue of this marriage was Durvinita who annexed Punnâḍ to the kingdom of the Gaṅgas.

Durvinita (605 to 650 A. D.) is known "as having his broad chest embraced, of her own accord, by the goddess of sovereignty, though she was intended by his father for another son", as the victor in the battles of Andari, Âlattûr, Poluḷaṟe, Pernagara (in Salem district); as the lord of Paṇṇâḍa and Punnâḍa; as the author of three works, namely a Śabdâvatâra, a saṇskṛit version of the Vaḍḍakatha or Bṛihatkatha, and a commentary on the 15th sarga of the Kirâtârjuniya (Mysore Archæol. Report, for 1916, page 45).

SYNCHRONIZZATION OF THE DYNASTIES OF THE DECCAN.

Circ. A.D.	Pallavas	Vakatakas	Vishnukundins	Kadambas	Gangas
425-450	Vîravarman	Pravarasêna II.		Kâkustha	Konkanivarman
450-475	Skandavarman				Mâdhava I.
		A son / Narêndrasêna	Mâdhava I.	Sântivarman / Krishnavarman I.	
475-500	Simhavarman / Y.M. Vishnugôpa	Dêvasêna / Prithivishêna II.	Vikramêndra I.	Mrigêsa / Vishnuvarman	Ayyavarman / Harivarman
500-525	Skandavarman / Simhavarman	Harishêna	Indrabhatharaka	Ravivarman / Simhavarman	Mâdhava / Vishnugôpa
525-550	Nandivarman / Vishnugôpa		Vikramêndra II.	Harivarmam / Krishnavarman. II	Krishnavarman / Mâdhava II.

Pravarasêna II being the grandson of Chandra-Gupta II (375-413) was certainly living in the second quarter of the V century.

The box-headed alphabets of the Kadamba kings Mrigêsa and Mândhatri are contemporaneous with the box-headed alphabet of the Balaghat plates of Prithivishêna II who was the son of a Kadamba (Kuntala) princess.

The Uruvupalli plates of Yuvamahârâja Vishnugôpa are box-headed as the plates of the Kadamba kings Mrigêsa and Mândhatri.

The alphabets of the Bendigānhalli (Mysore Arch. Rep. for 1914-15, plate XVIII) Chikkulla (Ep. Ind. Vol. IV, p. 196) and Bannahalli (Ep. Ind. Vol. VI., p. 18) plates are so similar that there is no room for doubting that the Ganga Krishnavarman, the Vishnukundin Vikramêndravarman II and the Kadamba Krishnavarman II were contemporaneous; the sister of this latter king married the Ganga Mâdhava II.

It is very probable that the Kadamba Harivarman ascended the throne in 537 A. D. and so, was contemporaneous with the Pallava king Vishnugôpa (525-550), grand father of Simhavishnu whose date 575-600 is not doubtful.

§ 3. The Châḷukyas.

The genealogy and the chronology of the Western Châḷukyas present no difficulty :

Jayasiṁha (of the Mânavya gôtra)
|
Raṇarâga
|
Raṇavikrama Puḷakêśin I (circ. 550 A. D.)
|
- Kîrtivarman I (566-597),
  - Puḷakêśin II., (609-642)
  - Kubjâ-Vishṇuvardhana (founder of the Eastern Châḷukya dynasty)
- Maṅgalêśa (597-608),

The origin of this dynasty is obscure [the legend given in the "grant of Vira-Choḍa," S. I. I., Vol. I., page 50, has nothing historical in it]. In 1905, (J. R. A. S., for 1905, page 360) Fleet found out that the hypotheses formed on this subject were all of them baseless. I shall, however, make a remark : the grant of Uṇḍivâṭika (Ep. Ind., Vol. VIII., page 163) which is probably dated in the first half of the VI century says that the commander of the fort of Harivâtsakoṭṭa was a certain Jayasiṁha (see also Ind. Ant., Vol XXX). Can this Jayasiṁha be the founder of the Châḷukya dynasty ?

Puḷakêśin I., who probably came from a town called Indukânti installed himself about 550 A. D., at Vâtâpi (Bâdâmi). We have said that this military operation could have been effected only by having defeated the Kadamba king (probably Harivarman) who reigned, with Halsi for capital, over the modern provinces of Kaladgee, Belgaum, and Dharwar. The historical documents say that he performed a horse sacrifice. We know also (Bâdâmi insc., Ind. Ant., Vol. III, page 305; Vol. VI, page 363; Vol. X, page 58) that he married Durlabhadêvi of the Batpûra family. This family lived probably not far from Goa at Rêvatîdvîpa (Goa plates; J. B. B. R. A. S., Vol. X., page 348). His eldest son Kîrtivarman I. succeeded him in 566-7 A. D.

The inscription of Mahâkûṭa (near Bâdâmi) [Ind. Ant., Vol. XIX, page 7] says that Kîrtivarman gained victories in the following countries : Vaṅga and Aṅga (E. and W. Bengal), Kaḷiṅga, Vaṭṭûra, Magadha, Madraka, Kêraḷa, Gaṅga, Mûshaka, Pâṇḍya, Dramiḷa, Chôḷiya, Âḷuka (the Âluvas or Âlupas, in the N.-E of Banavâsi) and Vijayantî. Again, the Aihole inscription says that Kirtivarman was a "night of doom to the Naḷas, the Mauryas and the Kadambas." The Naḷas probably occupied Naḷavâdi (mentioned in plates of Vikramâditya I) near Bellary and Karnûl districts. The Mauryas were a people of Northern Koṅkan (see Bombay Gazetteer, Vol. I, Part. II., page 282). A stone discovered at Vâda in the Thâna district (see Bombay Gazetteer, Vol. XIV, page 373) mentions the Maurya Seketuvarman. We have already spoken of the defeat of the Kadambas a little before 570 A. D. It would appear that Kîrtivarman defeated a confedaration of Kadamba princes probably Kṛishṇavarman II and his feudatories. In the 12th year of his reign, Kîrtivarman had as Yuvamahârâja his young brother Maṅgalêśa; and it is this prince that had one of the caves of Bâdâmi dug in the year 500 of the Śaka era, which corresponds to 578 A. D. (Ind. Ant., Vol. III, page 305 ; Vol. VI, page 363; Vol. X, page 58). Kîrtivarman married a princess of the Sêndraka family who was the daughter of Sênânanda râja (Chipḷûṇ plates, Ep. Ind., Vol. III, page 51). Of this union was born a son named Puḷakêśin II. This prince was probably very young when his father died and the crown passed to Maṅgalêśa, the brother (or half-brother, Ind. Ant., Vol. XIX., page 15) of Kîrtivarman I.

The inscription of Mahâkûṭa which is dated in the 5th year of the reign of Maṅgalêśa i-e. 601-602 A. D. say (Ind. Ant., Vol. XIX, page 7) that this king vanquished Buddha, and the Nerûr plates (Ind. Ant., Vol. VII., page 166) say that he "put to flight Śaṁkaragaṇa's son Buddharâja and killed Swâmirâja of the Châlikya family (see also Ind. Ant., Vol. VI, page 363). We have already spoken of the defeat of Buddharâja when studying the Kaḷachuri dynasty. The Aihoḷe inscription (Ep.

Ind., Vol. VI, No. 1, page 8) says that Mañgalêśa "took in marriage the Fortune of the Kaṭachchuris" and seized upon the isle of Rêvatî ; it was perhaps in this island that Swâmirâja reigned. The Aihoḷe inscription adds : "when his elder brother's son named Polakêśin had formed the resolution to wander abroad as an exile, that Mañgalêśa abandoned together with the effort to secure the kingdom for his own son, both his kingdom and his life". This event took place in 608 A. D. Puḷakêśin was formally crowned in the following year.

The Aihoḷe inscription (Ep. Ind. Vol. VI, page 4) gives us the following description of the exploits of Puḷakêśin II.

Two chiefs, Âppâyika and Gôvinda having tried to conquer the country to the north of the river Bhima, one is repulsed and the other submits and becomes the ally of the Châḷukyas. Pulakêśin then lays siege to Vanavâsî and subdues the Gañgas, the Âḷupas who reigned in this region, as also the Mauryas of Koṅkan. He then besieges Purî, an important town on the coast of the western ocean (Arabian sea) ; the Lâṭas, the Mâḷavas and the Gûrjaras surrender as well as the inhabitants of the Vindhyas, the banks of the Rèvâ and the three Mahârâshṭras. In the North-east, Puḷakêśin subdues the kingdoms of Kaliṅga and Kôsaḷa. He seizes the citadel of Pishṭapura and fights near the waters of the Kunâḷa ; then he turns to the south, routs the king of the Pallavas (Mahêndravarman I.) of Kâñchi, crosses the Kàvêrî, causes "prosperity to the Chôḷas, Kêralas, Pâṇḍyas" and returns to his capital Bâdâmi. These exploits took place at the beginning of his reign, circ. 609 A. D. The conquest of the Telugu country comprising the districts of Godavari, Krishna and Guntur is a landmark in the history of the Deccan, owing to the creation of an important kingdom, that of the Eastern Châḷukyas.

It is noteworthy that the Aihole inscription which bears the date 634 A. D. makes no mention of king Harsha Vardhana. The documents posterior to it mention the victory gained by Puḷakêśin over Harsha. It is probable that it was about the year 636 A. D. that Harsha vanquished Dhruvasêna II, king of Valabhi ; Harsha wished to extend his conquests much more, but was stopped by Puḷakêśin. This event probably took place about 637 or 638 A. D.

We close the "Ancient History of the Deccan" with the year 610 A. D. At this epoch, Puḷakeśin II. has become master of the whole of the Deccan ; the Pallavas have been repulsed in the south, and all the other old dynasties have been destroyed. From 610 A. D. the documents have become more numerous, and chronology has become more precise ; we enter into a new epoch in the history of the Deccan, the middle ages.

Pondicherry, December 1919.

CONTENTS.